An Agnostic's Path to God

An Agnostic's Path to God

Gary L. Gaines

Copyright © 2016 Gary L. Gaines
All rights reserved.

ISBN: 1530513618
ISBN 13: 9781530513611

Library of Congress Control Number: 2016904362
CreateSpace Independent Publishing Platform
North Charleston, South Carolina

*To my wife, Darlene
Who is strong and true
And could teach the angels
A thing or two*

Table of Contents

Preface xv
Introduction xix
    When I Say *God* xxii
    Political Correctness xxiii
    Qualifying Statements xxiii
    Holy Books xxvi
    Tactical Overview xxix
    Public Opinion and God xxx
    A Little Personal Analysis xxxii
    This Is Not a Technical Book xxxiii

One   Logic 1
    Fact or Faith 1
    Belief Is Not Reality 2
    Free Will 4
    Problems with Miracles 5
    Man Invents God 7
    Speaking of Sin 8
    Power to Spare 10
    Heaven Cannot Wait 11

	Not a Choice · 12
	A Perfect Mess · 13
	The Elusive Soul · 15
	Can We Believe What We Read · · · · · · · · · · · 17
	Where Did the Wisdom Come From · · · · · · · 18
	Where Did the Devil Come From · · · · · · · · · 19
	Role Model · 20
	Let Us Get Personal · 20
	What We Think · 21
	Is God Good · 22
	God and Hell · 23
	Problems in Paradise · 23
	Peer Pressure · 24
	Divine Design or Dice · · · · · · · · · · · · · · · · · · 25
	Dragons in Utah · 26
	God and the Eons · 27
	God's Home away from Home · · · · · · · · · · · · 29
	Telewhat · 30
	God in the Gaps · 31
	No Pain, No Gain · 32
	Religion and Morality · · · · · · · · · · · · · · · · · · · 33
	The Fine-Tuning Argument · · · · · · · · · · · · · · 35
Two	Religion 1 · 40
	What Keeps Us Apart · · · · · · · · · · · · · · · · · · · 40
	What about Jesus, Muhammad, and Others · · 42
	No Hell for Me · 43
	Who Is in Charge · 43

	Why Apologize · · · · · · · · · · · · 44
	What Are the Odds · · · · · · · · · · 45
	A Little Prayer · · · · · · · · · · · · 47
	What Is the Difference · · · · · · · · 47
	The Big Mo · · · · · · · · · · · · · · 49
	A Mind Is a Terrible Thing to Waste · · · · 50
	The Big Promise · · · · · · · · · · · · 51
	A Constant Wonder · · · · · · · · · · 52
	Women and Children · · · · · · · · · · 53
	Cherry-Picking for the Bible · · · · · · · 54
	Terrorism 101 · · · · · · · · · · · · · 55
	Jewish Claim to Israel · · · · · · · · · 55
	Morality or Obedience · · · · · · · · · 56
	The Meat of the Matter · · · · · · · · · 57
	The Second Creation · · · · · · · · · · 59
	No Clear Winner · · · · · · · · · · · · 61
	Come Judgment Day · · · · · · · · · · 62
	The Power of Dogma · · · · · · · · · · 63
	Self-Serving · · · · · · · · · · · · · · 63
	Judge Not · · · · · · · · · · · · · · · 64
	How We See Things · · · · · · · · · · 65
Three	Religion 2 · · · · · · · · · · · · · · · 68
	My Way Okay · · · · · · · · · · · · · 68
	Death in Design · · · · · · · · · · · · 69
	What the Commandments Command · · · · · · 71
	Choices, Choices · · · · · · · · · · · · 73
	No Church for Agnostics · · · · · · · · · 73

	Faith and Love · 74
	Religious Bullying · 74
	Two Wrongs · 76
	God Is What · 76
	No Pets Allowed · 77
	The Myth Goes On · 78
	What Preachers Preach · · · · · · · · · · · · · · · · · 79
	Sin and Guilt · 80
	God's Will · 81
	Priorities · 82
	The Troublesome Tenth · · · · · · · · · · · · · · · · · 83
	Trouble with Angels · · · · · · · · · · · · · · · · · · · 84
	Religion the Easy Way · · · · · · · · · · · · · · · · · · 85
	More Than We Can Handle · · · · · · · · · · · · · · 86
	Chaos and Change · 86
	The Chosen Few · 87
	Democracy and a Supreme Being · · · · · · · · · · 87
	Bankruptcy · 89
	Familiarity Breeds Reality · · · · · · · · · · · · · · · 90
	It Is No Sacrifice · 91
Four	Christianity · 93
	Why Die for Me · 94
	Looks Can Be Deceiving · · · · · · · · · · · · · · · · 97
	What Purpose Hell · 98
	Immaculate Conception(s) · · · · · · · · · · · · · · 98
	Papal Power · 99
	Mono What · 100

	The Question of Resurrection	101
	Resurrection Part II	104
	Jesus and Prophecies	105
	Poor Ol' Judas and Others	106
	Secret Miracles	107
	Mass Appeal	107
	Is Doubting Wrong	109
	We All Need One	110
	My Dilemma	110
Five	Science	112
	Test of Time	112
	Where Do We Come From	113
	Mortal Clouds	115
	Evolution 101	115
	Time, Place, and Copernicus	119
	Lead Me Not into It	120
	Copernicus Revisited	121
	Little Green Men and the Bible	122
	What Is Life	123
	Life-after-Death Musings	124
	Dating	125
	A Quantum Fluctuation	126
	Quantum Quivers	128
	It Is about Time	129
	More Religious Bashing	131
	Time Revisited	132
	The Appeal of Evolution	134

	Who Can You Trust · · · · · · · · · · · · · · 135
	Genes for God · · · · · · · · · · · · · · · · 135
	More on Hardwired for Religion · · · · · · · · 136
	What about Tomorrow · · · · · · · · · · · · · 137
	Laws of Nature · · · · · · · · · · · · · · · · 138
	Digital Musings · · · · · · · · · · · · · · · · 139
	A Word about Consciousness · · · · · · · · · · 140
	The Next Challenge · · · · · · · · · · · · · · 143
	The Logic of an Agnostic · · · · · · · · · · · 144
Six	What I Believe · · · · · · · · · · · · · · · · 145
	Moral Issues · · · · · · · · · · · · · · · · · 146
	Social Issues · · · · · · · · · · · · · · · · · 147
	Personal Issues · · · · · · · · · · · · · · · · 149
	Philosophical Issues · · · · · · · · · · · · · · 150
Seven	What I Want · · · · · · · · · · · · · · · · · · 154
	I Want a God · · · · · · · · · · · · · · · · · 154
	I Want a Religion · · · · · · · · · · · · · · · 157
	I Want Heaven Too · · · · · · · · · · · · · · 159
Eight	What I Have · · · · · · · · · · · · · · · · · · 161
	I Have Hope · · · · · · · · · · · · · · · · · 162
	I Have Imagination · · · · · · · · · · · · · · 163
	The Epiphany · · · · · · · · · · · · · · · · · 164
	What about the Logic of an Agnostic · · · · · · 166
	You Too Can Find a Path · · · · · · · · · · · · 167
	God Is · 169
	My God · 171
	Where Is the Logic · · · · · · · · · · · · · · 173

	Why Do It · 174
	What It Means · 176
	East Meets West · 177
	What about the Churches · · · · · · · · · · · · · · · 178
	Summary · 180
	An Agnostic's Path to God · · · · · · · · · · · · · · 182
Nine	What I Think Is Next · · · · · · · · · · · · · · · · · · · 183
	Epilogue · 187

Preface

This book took me down a path I did not expect.

I started out describing the flaws of logic I felt were associated with belief in the God of Abraham. I called the book *The Logic of an Agnostic* because that is what it was all about. But then it became something different. It took me down a path to a god and an afterlife unlike those associated with the God of Abraham. It became *An Agnostic's Path to God*.

Most of my life I have wondered about god (both the supreme being worshipped by Christians, Muslims, and Jews, and other possible gods). Does one (or more) exist? If so, where did this god come from? Is he or she good? Is he or she omnipotent? Why do most people accept the existence of a god as fact when I am unsure? How can belief in the supernatural have such a profound influence on individuals, societies, and governments? All my questioning led to doubts, causing me to be ambivalent about the god that most people believe in. Perhaps a more accurate statement would be to say I am an agnostic. I just do not know.

I wanted to explain why I am an agnostic, so I wrote down a lot of reasons why belief in the Abrahamic god seems illogical to me. I arranged the reasons in chapters to provide organization. But after I had written a few chapters, my thinking took me in a different direction. I first listed some of my basic beliefs, and then I wrote a chapter describing the god, religion, and heaven I want. That got me to thinking about a relationship that almost anyone could have with a god, which led to a chapter on how I, and others, could find a path to the god we want. Finally, I concluded with a chapter on what I think heaven would be like.

I believe most people would find this book entertaining and informative. I think all will see that I am not anti-religious. I am just a simple person searching for answers. And I think most people, religious or not, would enjoy reading it to learn about the logic and beliefs of an agnostic. Or to see how the god, religion, and heaven I want are described. Or to see how everyone can find a god. Or even to see how heaven can be imagined by an agnostic.

My all-time favorite quote, and one that started me down the path to discovering my own god, is from an unknown source and has been around for a long time: "We don't see things as they are. We see things as we are." Therefore, I know you will see most of this book as you are, and that is okay. But maybe, if I am lucky, you will see some of my logic and a little of how I feel the future could be.

Introduction

Entwined in the definition of religion is wording like "a specific system of belief, often involving a code of ethics." If you focus on that part of the definition, I am religious. I have a belief system, and ethics are involved. But I am not religious to the extent of accepting the "specific system of belief" of any organized religion that I have explored, including, among others, Christianity, Judaism, Islam, Buddhism, and Hinduism. And I am not religious to the extent of accepting the god referred to in the most popular god-based religions. It would be wrong to say I am an atheist because even though I do not accept a god as most people do, I do acknowledge the concept of god and do not profess to know if one or more exist. Many people would likely call me a secular humanist, but I think agnostic fits best.

I started this book to explain why I do not accept God as most people do. I wanted to put my reasons in writing to show that I have given this a lot of thought, to force myself to express my thoughts with clarity, and to provide a record of why I believe as I do. Most of the reasons are not original. They come from my readings on religion, science, logic, philosophy, and other related subjects, and from listening to and observing others. But some of the reasons are original; at least I have not heard them before. I will not deny that some of the reasons are petty, but I think many of them are important, and some are even profound. Each one, petty or not, plays a part in why I feel as I do, and all are in my own words.

Some themes, such as those about good, evil, omnipotence, the origin of the universe, and others, appear in more than one reason. However, the themes are used to make a different point or are discussed from a different perspective each time in ways that I believe make the statements in each reason unique. I try not to be wordy or repetitive because I do not like reading such material myself.

The reasons are not intended as an attack on the Bible or the Quran. The accuracy and content of both have been discussed by a multitude of scholars over the ages, and I am not qualified, nor is it my intent, to repeat or expand on those discussions. My reasons relate to the logic of religious beliefs or how consistent those beliefs are with the reality I perceive. Nor are the reasons meant as an attack on religion or religious people; instead, they simply represent my questioning or understanding of the issue being discussed. I do respect everyone's right to be religious, and I even envy the comfort that religion can provide. However, I feel that many religious beliefs are absurd, illogical, contrived, or otherwise flawed and contribute to or promote inappropriate behavior by corrupting the mind of the believer. Details on such flaws are provided in various parts of the book.

I sometimes use the words *god, religion, god-based religion, religious beliefs*, and similar terms synonymously. I try to be concise in my wording, but in some cases, I think the terms are pretty much interchangeable, and I do not think such usage distracts from my overall point.

The reasons I have trouble believing in God are divided into four categories and covered in five chapters: Logic, Religion (1 and 2), Christianity, and Science. Some of the reasons did not fit well in any of these categories, but I felt some organization was needed, and these seemed to work best. (I explain later why a separate chapter is provided on Christianity.) The last four chapters cover what I believe, what I want, what I have, and what I think is next. Some poems are included, if you can call them that, at random locations.

Before starting on the reasons, I explain what I mean when I refer to god, I make a brief comment about political correctness, I offer some qualifying statements, and I make some comments about the holy books. I also explain my tactics, make a few comments about public opinion and God, and offer a little personal analysis to help explain why

I believe as I do. I end the introduction with brief comments about the overall nature of the book.

When I Say *God*

I know the concept of a supreme being means different things to different people, and I know different names are used to refer to a supreme being, including God, Jehovah, Allah, Elohim, Yahweh, Lord, and others. Some even feel God is too undefinable to denote with a name, and some use a metaphor or symbol to refer to God. When I say *God* in this book, usually I mean the God of the Quran and the Bible, which is the God of the Muslims, Christians, and Jews and the various cults and sects associated with each. This God is sometimes called the Abrahamic god, since the Muslims, Christians, and Jews all trace their beliefs to the patriarch Abraham. According to the holy books, God chose Abraham to father his people, and Abraham had two sons: Ishmael, by Hagar, whose descendants include the Arab people and Muhammad; and Ishmael's stepbrother, Isaac, by Sarah, whose descendants include the Hebrews and Jesus.

When writing about religion in the context that I do, I do not think it is necessary to use a multitude of names for God to distinguish among different belief systems. Certainly to do so would be unwieldy, and I do not think clarity would be gained. Therefore, I will just use the word *God* to mean the Abrahamic god, or the god of the Bible and Quran. Again, I know the Bible and Quran do not embrace the exact same concept of a supreme being, but I believe there are enough similarities that I can simply say God and not cause confusion. I take this liberty as a convenience and sincerely do not mean to ignore or diminish the uniqueness of anyone's belief system.

I capitalize the word *God* when clearly referring to the Abrahamic god and use lowercase for god elsewhere. Sometimes the distinction is not real clear, so please forgive me if I err.

Political Correctness

I use male pronouns when referring to any god. I also use male pronouns or gender-free references when gender is unknown. (I find the use of "he/she" or the like cumbersome.) I take these liberties for convenience and consistency. I am not a sexist, and I hope my use of the male pronouns does not offend anyone. As I say elsewhere, the Abrahamic religions are sexist, and I certainly do not want to contribute to that prejudice.

Qualifying Statements

These comments are not meant to be unequivocally anti-God but as anti-God based on my understanding of God. I offer the comments not in an attempt to diminish anyone's belief but simply to try to explain why I believe as I do. I struggle to find answers to life's big questions, and by putting the reasons for my struggle in writing, I force myself to follow a structured thought process. I realize my beliefs are based to some extent on ignorance because I have no training in theology, except for personal study. (This may be an advantage because I do not feel obligated to support any religious position.) But I remain open-minded, and if I discover information that is more compelling than what I now have, or if I find that statements made herein are wrong, my beliefs will change.

I raise questions about religious matters not from a desire to belittle or destroy religion but because that is where my thinking takes me. I am not anti-religious. I did not decide one day to do all I could to be anti-religious. I simply found that I could not accept the religious beliefs as I understand them, so I thought that if I could put my doubts in words, I might gain understanding. What better way to gain knowledge and insight is there than to be very candid and specific about one's doubts? Acceptance does not advance thinking, and conformity does not provide insight.

Although I do not accept most religious beliefs as truth or as a valid representation of reality, I consider myself religious. I believe in the possibility of a supreme being. I pray regularly. I have a rigid belief system that includes the non-proselytizing commandments from the Bible, as well as the golden rule and other religious-like teachings. I fear death and would like to believe that there is life after death in a wonderful place with family, friends, acquaintances, and others.

Some people were taught to believe a certain way from childhood, and they accept the teachings as fact. Good for them. Some people come to religion later in life and cling to it as absolute. Good for them. I envy the comfort their beliefs give them and would like to feel that comfort myself. But I have always questioned things that do not seem logical. I cannot help it. I do not necessarily like it, but it is the way I am. If accepting things based on faith had a switch, I might turn it on, because there is little joy in not knowing.

But I hope that by writing about my doubts, about things concerning religion that I find illogical, false, or dubious, I might forge a path to a religious-like reality I can accept. And I believe I have started down that path because I have learned a lot in trying to put my doubts in words, even to the point of thinking there may be something beyond the physical chaos I see as reality. By *something* I mean an intangible beyond the physical—an intangible beyond the protons, neutrons, and electrons, beyond the molecules, galaxies, and universe(s) that help shape our reality. I do not believe that intangible is the result of mystical beliefs conjured up thousands of years ago; instead I believe it is the mental side of what we humans contribute to the reality we experience.

I muse more about the mental side of religion later in the book, and that is where I discover a path to a personal god that I had not expected. I believe most of us, religious or not, create the god we want in our minds. If we follow a traditional religion, that god is probably similar to the Abrahamic god, but if we are not Christian, Muslim, or Jewish, that god is probably more like what we want in a god. In either case, I think a lot of religious belief stems from a process of mental creation and therefore knows few boundaries. Thus, I believe we can use this creative process to forge a path to a god that is free of restrictions and open to all. I did not set out with this path in mind. In fact, it came as a surprise, but it is where my thoughts and writing took me.

I think there is a lot of good in the world, and good is synonymous with the god I want. There is good everywhere I look. I know there is bad too. I think some bad is inevitable. But good is a gift. And when I say *good*, I mean things like love, affection, beauty, empathy, charity, happiness, smiles, open minds, science, math, self-control, responsibility, values without bias, the desire to do good, and probably a million other things I have left out.

Holy Books

The Bible and the Quran are holy books to billions of religious people and provide the basis of what we know about God. Christians embrace both the Old and New Testaments of the Bible. Jews embrace the Old Testament, especially the first five books, known as the Pentateuch or Torah. And the Muslims embrace the Quran. I have read and studied both the Bible and the Quran but must confess I am more familiar with the Bible because I was raised in a predominately Christian society and was not exposed to Islam until later in life. (Muslims are included in this discussion primarily because theirs is an Abrahamic god, and many of their beliefs do have commonality with those of the Christians and Jews.)

The Bible was written by different people at different times and then compiled and revised by different people at different times, all without consistent, authoritative control of the contents; therefore, present versions may be substantially different from the original writings. In contrast, the Quran came from a single source, and present versions are thought to be very similar to the original because rigorous oversight of oral and written reproductions has occurred. From the time the angel Gabriel is thought to have revealed the Quran to Muhammad, contents were passed along by reciters and scribes who were subjected to great scrutiny. There is some controversy related to the existence of multiple versions of the Quran early on, along with missing, revised, and contradictory verses, but I believe it is fair to say that the holy book of Islam has not been revised since its inception to nearly the same degree as the Bible. I do not know how relevant this is because I feel all religions, regardless of the documents they are based on, are inventions of man.

Gary L. Gaines

The Old Testament of the Bible and the Quran have some similarities. Both refer to some of the same prophets (for example, Abraham, Isaac, Jacob, Lot, Noah, Jonah, and Moses), and both talk of heaven and hell. However, the main difference between the Bible and the Quran is the assertion in the New Testament of the Bible that Jesus Christ was the Messiah. The Quran does not accept Jesus as the Messiah. The Quran has high praise for Jesus but calls him a prophet, not a messiah. The Quran disputes that Jesus was the son of God and labels the concept blasphemous. And the Quran asserts that belief in God, the son of God, and the Holy Spirit is polytheism. Since the Quran seeks to correct and clarify parts of the Bible, an understanding of the Bible is necessary to understand the Quran. In fact, I think it is fair to say that an understanding of each book facilitates an understanding of the other.

I am not qualified to compare the Bible and the Quran in detail, but I offer these broad generalizations: Parts of both books are hard to read and understand, but I believe the Bible is more readable and literary. Also, the Bible is more of a historical document, spanning thousands of years, with many beautiful stories, strong, charismatic figures, and diverse styles. It was written by several individuals over a wide span of time. The Quran is more instructive and direct and does not follow a chronology, and it came through a single prophet during a relatively short period of time. The Quran claims to be the final and perfect word or Allah, as dictated to the holy prophet Muhammad.

An Agnostic's Path to God

The Old Testament of the Bible contains a lot of violence and bloodshed and portrays an unforgiving attitude, whereas the New Testament is more about peace, acceptance, forgiveness, grace, and faith. The Quran is absolute in its support of Allah, and its tone varies from one of tolerance, forgiveness, and altruism to one that promotes violence. Both the Bible and the Quran talk of life after death for those who meet certain criteria, and both contain principles to live by that would serve anyone well, but both also contain material that only the faithful could accept.

Tactical Overview

Usually when people question whether there is a god, they use one of two general tactics: They either list attributes they think a god would have and then question whether such attributes are possible, either individually or in combination with each other, or they question whether the reality they perceive is consistent with the existence of a god. I am not keen on the first tactic. I believe if there is a god, he is impossible for us to define. Certainly he would have some supernatural attributes, but to say that he is omnipotent, omniscient, immutable, omnipresent, benevolent, and so forth, and then to question whether it is possible to possess such attributes, either individually or in combination, seems a little disingenuous and pedantic to me. We cannot define a supernatural entity, and if there were one, we certainly could not assess his inner workings.

Therefore, for the most part, this text questions whether our reality is consistent with the existence of the Abrahamic god. Supernatural attributes are mentioned but only in the context of the subject being discussed. The ability of a being to possess supernatural attributes is not questioned. The questions raised herein relate more to whether our reality reflects the application of such attributes.

Further, some people and organizations question or criticize religion by lampooning religious leaders or otherwise being disrespectful to religious beliefs. I do not agree with those tactics. Obviously I agree with challenging religious beliefs, but I believe this can be done without being disrespectful. Cartoons or other despicable characterizations of religious icons or doctrines are divisive and do little to change minds. If something as personal and profound as religion is to be challenged, I believe it must be done using logic and structured thought in a deliberate, respectful way. As I have said elsewhere, I do not agree with a lot of religious beliefs, but I do respect religious people, and I would not purposely be disrespectful to them.

Public Opinion and God

Public opinion surveys indicate that more than 90 percent of Americans believe in God, and the percentage has stayed consistent since the 1950s, when polls on the matter were first conducted. This is incredible! With Supreme Court rulings beginning around that time that struck down classroom religious instructions, school-sponsored prayer, mandatory Bible reading, and antievolution laws in public schools; with huge strides in biology, quantum mechanics, cosmology, astronomy, and many other areas of science; and with the increases in our standard of living and education level, one would think that belief would have decreased, but it did not. The staying power of belief in God in the face of such headwinds is truly amazing.

I know public opinion does not create reality, and longevity is not necessarily synonymous with truth. And maybe some people do not really believe in God but do not want to admit that to pollsters. Maybe some people just did not give it much thought but answered yes when asked because that is traditional. But even so, with religion pretty much removed from public schools, with better science to explain reality, and with reduced poverty and ignorance, one would expect belief in god to decrease. But it has not. Not at all.

I offer many reasons in this book for being an agnostic. I have tried to base my arguments on logic, and if I stay true to that theme, logic tells me that most people in the United States sincerely do believe in the god of Abraham. Even if the percentage is not exactly right, the polls have it so high that it is logical to believe that the overwhelming majority of Americans believe in God. I think this is amazing.

Gary L. Gaines

A Little Personal Analysis

Why do more than 90 percent of the people in this country differ significantly from me regarding belief in God? I think there are at least three reasons. First, I was not raised in a religious household. I had a little exposure to religion because I sometimes went to church with my grandparents when I was a kid. Also, I recall the teacher reading Bible stories when I went to a two-room country school in the early grades. But my parents were not religious and never talked about religion. (I know my father was somewhat anti-religious, because he sometimes mentioned that his father was very religious and had tried to make him that way, which had made him resent religion at an early age.)

Second, I have always been leery of subjects that are based primarily on subjective information because I feel such information is biased. I do not distrust people. I think most people are honest. But I believe people rationalize to the extent that they do not see their thinking as biased. Anyway, I am just not able to give much credibility to subjective information on most issues. (I even distrust a lot of what is reported as fact. I see spin and bias almost everywhere.)

Third, and perhaps most important, the reality I perceive conflicts with what is described in the holy books—not just in the supernatural parts but in the way God is portrayed also. If God is real, I know we mortals cannot understand or characterize him. But even so, I just cannot believe he would act as described. The supernatural parts of the Abrahamic religions take a lot of faith to believe, but to me, the way God's behavior is described takes even more.

I think my upbringing, my suspicion of subjective information, and my perception of reality prevent me from believing in the God of Christians, Muslims, and Jews. I do not necessarily like being this way, but as Popeye the Sailor Man said many years ago, "I yam what I yam."

This Is Not a Technical Book

There are no footnotes, minimal quotes, and few technical references. My aim was to use logic and self-evident statements to make my points and stimulate thinking. The few technical matters cited are explained in the text. I did a lot of research and tried very hard to be technically correct, and nowhere did I purposely misrepresent, slant, or misstate any information.

I like technical books, but I wanted this to be lighter, simpler, and shorter, with beliefs, thoughts, opinions, and ideas to entertain and stimulate, not necessarily to change minds. I know that changing minds on religious issues is like getting an elephant to dance with a squirrel: It is just not likely to happen. I set out to question the logic of the Abrahamic religions and ended up on a path to a god who is related, yet very different.

Finally, I truly enjoyed writing this book. I really like reading, thinking, and writing about religious issues. And if only one other person finds some value in what I have written, my satisfaction will be doubled.

One

Logic

The first reasons why I doubt the existence of God are based primarily on logic. In this sense I mean logic as a thought process based on correct reasoning or what could be expected by the working of cause and effect. I know that logic can be somewhat subjective. Different people may define *correct* in different ways and may conclude different effects from the same cause. But I have tried to be true to the process of objective reasoning and sincerely hope that even for those who may not agree with me, my struggle for truth is apparent.

Fact or Faith

We have no rational proof that there is a god. No objective analyses point to the existence of a god. Belief in God is based primarily on faith, which is subjective, personal, and arbitrary. Faith is not something anyone can choose or learn. It is an emotion that a person either feels or does not. Faith is not fact in the sense that it can be proved by objective, analytical data, by a logical extension of facts, or by cause-and-effect reasoning.

Having a belief based on faith is significant to whoever has the faith, but may mean little to someone without the faith. Consider all the many kinds of religions in the world: Each has meaning to its followers but may mean little to others. Does a Christian find deep meaning in the teachings of Buddha? Does a Jew accept the significance of the New Testament? Does a Muslim believe Jesus was the Messiah?

Religious faith can be extremely strong, as evidenced by the actions of some religious people. It can cause people to love, to hate, or to feel a myriad of emotions in between. It can drive them to do great deeds or hideous atrocities. But faith is not necessarily a manifestation of a logical thought process. It is driven by something other than logic, and the emotions and deeds that result are often beyond logical explanation.

Belief Is Not Reality
People believe in God for many reasons:

- Some believe because they have been taught to believe.
- Some believe because they find security in trusting a power higher than man.

- Some believe because they find comfort in rote and tradition.
- Some believe because they want answers to questions that humans cannot answer.
- Some believe because they want to conform.
- Some believe because they fear the finality of death.
- Some believe because they cannot accept the chaotic nature of reality.
- And certainly there are many other reasons people believe in God.

While none of the reasons are necessarily wrong or bad, none provide a factual basis for believing there is a god. The act or emotion of believing does not necessarily have any relation to the reality of what is believed. For example, at one time most people, even educated people, believed the earth was flat. Of course that did not make the earth flat. On a personal level, many people have believed in the integrity of a friend or loved one, only to learn later that such belief was ill founded. This often leads to broken friendships, divorces, or estrangement of some other kind.

In short, belief in something does not necessarily make it so. Most of the world's religious people believe in God; however, that does not make God a reality. I am not necessarily asserting that billions of people are wrong. I am just asserting that we do not know for certain that they are right. Reality is not a product of popularity, faith, belief, or desire. Reality is the way things are, not necessarily the way we want them to be.

Free Will

Do people have free will? And if they do, does that explain why there is evil in the world? If people do have free will, and some choose to do evil deeds, at least two problems of logic arise. First is the question as to the omnipotence of God, and second is the implication that if people have free will, some will inevitably choose to do evil.

Regarding omnipotence, if God were omnipotent, when he created the universe, he could have created it any way he chose. If he had wanted to give people free will, he could have done so, even though doing so would have relinquished some of his future omnipotence by creating beings that he could not control. Also this raises an issue of logic: Can an omnipotent being create a situation that reduces his omnipotence? True omnipotence means unlimited power. But for whatever reason, maybe God did deliberately create beings that he could not control. Then the question becomes one of free will choosing evil.

It is not logical to assume that evil must inevitably exist among beings who have free will. Those who believe in God do not view him as evil, yet he has free will, showing that it is possible to have free will and not choose evil. Therefore, if

God were omnipotent and altogether good when he created the universe, he would have created beings in his image; that is, he would have created beings who had free will, but who would never choose evil. He would have created them such that they always freely chose to do the right thing. Perhaps the fact that evil exists shows that God is either not omnipotent or not altogether good.

Problems with Miracles

Some people believe in miracles. They believe there is a god and that he intervenes in earthly affairs to change what would otherwise be natural outcomes. They cite events from the past as evidence of miracles, and some even point to present-day events, such as when a very sick person recovers or when someone survives a bad accident. But the concept of miracles raises questions of logic.

One question of logic arises when miracles are cited as proof that God exists. It is not logical to use one thing that is questionable as proof of another thing that is equally questionable. It is not logical to say, "I believe miracles have occurred; therefore that proves that God exists." To believe in miracles is to believe in God. One is not proof of the other.

Miracles raise other problems too. If miracles do happen—that is, if there is a god, and he does sometimes intervene in earthly affairs by changing what would otherwise be natural outcomes—that means he is capricious. He intervenes in some instances and not in others. And such capriciousness would condition some people to ask for miracles and resent it if they did not happen. Also, tampering with natural outcomes creates an uncertainty and unpredictability as far as how humanity views the normal forces of nature. And if miracles do happen, they show that God can and will intervene in worldly affairs under certain conditions, which raises the question of why does he allow so much pain and evil to exist. He could intervene and make the world a better place for everybody all the time.

Either God intervenes in earthly affairs, or he does not. If he periodically performs miracles, then he is capricious. And that shows he could do more. If he does not intervene, then miracles do not happen, and there is no need to pray or to thank him for outcomes.

People will probably always refer to certain events as miracles, and most do so without meaning to be philosophical or religious. They are simply describing an event the best way they know how. But those who cite miracles as proof of the existence of God are putting him in a predicament. They are saying he periodically intervenes in human affairs, which means he is capricious. And they are saying he could do more, but chooses not to.

Man Invents God

The concept of god appears to be a human invention rather than a discovery of fact. We do not know when the concept of god or gods began, but it appears that ancient people had many fears, superstitions, spirits, and gods. It also appears that many of the multiple-god beliefs of our ancient ancestors eventually gave way to belief in a single god. Now the Jews, Muslims, and Christians embrace a single god, although the Christians believe that their god is represented by a holy trinity consisting of God; his son, Jesus; and the Holy Spirit. As the concept of god evolved, different religions developed with different belief systems related to the same or a similar god.

The different beliefs can be as trivial as the meaning of a specific word in the Bible or Quran or as significant as the personification of God on earth. The various god-based religions embrace vastly different beliefs that are based on the same or a similar god. This variety implies that the beliefs are subjective. And in fact, some major religious sects or cults are based on an individual person's interpretation of religious doctrine. And some are based on an individual's assertion that he or she received divine guidance through a sign or vision or some other personal interaction with God.

The resemblance of God to man is further indication that God is an invention of humans. The assertion is that God created man in his image. Therefore, when we look at religious images and art and other places where God is depicted, we are likely to see that white people have a white god, red people have a red god, black people have a black god, and so on. If intelligent beings were discovered on another planet, it is likely that they would have a god that resembles them. Again, this self-serving subjectivity portends an invented god rather than an actual one.

Once the concept of god is accepted, other inventions related to the concept follow. Some of the most common are the fable, fantasy, and myth associated with God; the concept of immortality and a human soul; and the various organized religions in general. And each organized religion has its own principles to defend, guide, and perpetuate its specific belief system.

History has shown that religious principles are subject to change based on new insights, interpretations, archeological discoveries, changes in public opinion, or other factors. And history has shown that new religious organizations can be formed, and existing ones can spin off new sects with different belief systems. These changes mean that the concept of god in the future may be very different from the concept held today, further implying that the beliefs are subjective to the point of being mundane.

Speaking of Sin
Sometimes sin is hard to pin down. Thou shalt not kill, but what about police or soldiers or executioners? Thou shalt not

steal, but what about a mother stealing bread for a starving child? Thou shalt not bear false witness, but what about a lie that spares feelings or saves lives? Honor thy father and thy mother, but what about parents who abuse their children? The point is, sin is somewhat subjective; therefore, to some extent the meaning of sin depends on how we view it or what is in our mind. Sin is not black and white. It is various shades of gray. Other than for sociopaths and others who are insensitive to the feelings of others, I think it is good that we determine the severity of sin based on our own standards or experiences. We should not go through life ignoring bad behavior, but we should not see sin in everything either. The original sin is an example of seeing too much sin.

Some believe certain passages from the Bible mean that sin in the Garden of Eden, referred to as the original sin, ancestral sin, or inherited sin, has an everlasting affect on all of humankind. (This does not apply to Muslims because the Quran does not contain such passages.) It is hard to see the logic of punishing humankind forever for things that may have happened thousands of years ago, but some feel our propensity to sin or feel guilt or even the fact that we all eventually die are a result of the original sin.

Some religious teachings, such as the non-proselytizing commandments and the golden rule, are good standards to live by. But logic tells me that the definition of sin is subjective, and we should therefore be very reluctant to judge others based on our own standard. Logic also tells me that it is good that we rationalize our sins to some extent because we should not go through life feeling remorse, depression, or guilt for things that are of little consequence or that we had nothing to do with.

Power to Spare
If there is a god, and he created the universe, his power is beyond comprehension. To bring all the mass and energy of the universe into existence, to make time pass and galaxies spin, to create light from darkness, to breathe life into clay, to create all that there is and ever will be demonstrates power and understanding that will be forever beyond us. Our minds could never comprehend or even touch the omnipotence of such a god. But if there were such a god, why would he kill children to carry out his plan?

It is not logical. A power that could call billions of stars into existence could get his way without taking the firstborn. A power that could create an eggplant and an elephant over and over could get his way without raining fire and brimstone. A power that could evoke the wonders of a human mind could get his way without threatening that mind. It is not logical to think that an omnipotent, benevolent god would kill, destroy, and intimidate to carry out his plan. His power would allow him to influence destiny without resorting to such crude methods, and his benevolence would prevent him from treating people that way. More than anything else, the biblical portrayal of God makes me a nonbeliever as far as the Abrahamic god is concerned. I just cannot accept a god who would act as described in the Bible.

Heaven Cannot Wait

Some people say they have seen heaven or visited heaven or had some experience that took them to heaven. Books have been written about such claims, and some seem credible. The experience often occurs when the person is near death and unconscious or semiconscious. Is it logical to believe that some people have visited heaven and have come back to tell about it? I think there are at least three reasons why the visits are not a representation of reality.

First, if there is a god and he is omnipotent, he does not make mistakes. He would not call someone to heaven by accident. I guess he could do it on purpose to give humanity a glimpse of what heaven is like, but he would know that anecdotal evidence is always questionable, and if he wanted to give humanity a glimpse of heaven, I do not think he would tease. I think he would find a way of doing so that was credible and believable to all.

Second, based on the holy books, there will be a judgment day when God picks those who will go to heaven. Granted, when someone dies, time is probably not relevant, so to those going to heaven, the transformation may seem instantaneous. But to the living, the near living, or the barely living, Judgment Day has not come yet. So for people to assert that they went to heaven before Judgment Day is not consistent with religious teachings and could be viewed as blasphemy.

And third, a more logical explanation is that those who say they went to heaven and came back were dreaming, embellishing, hallucinating, or fabricating. We know that people dream, and some embellish their dreams, and some of our dreams are so vivid that we have trouble distinguishing them from reality at a later date. And we know that people with high fever or under anesthesia can hallucinate and then confuse the hallucinations with reality when they recover. And of course we know that some people just plain lie.

But it does appear that some people truly believe they went to heaven and returned. I have read accounts that seemed to come from credible people. But belief does not create reality. And the accounts have not provided any new details about heaven. They repeat what has been conjectured about heaven for hundreds of years. Therefore, logic tells me that no one has actually gone to heaven and returned.

Not a Choice

It has been said that we have everything to gain and nothing to lose by believing in God. If he is real and we believe, we could reap great rewards; if he is not real and we believe, there is no penalty. Therefore, philosophers and laypeople alike have asked: Why take the chance? Why not accept God and be safe?

The flaw to this logic is that belief in God is not a choice. We may be predisposed to certain beliefs because of our heredity and our environment, but what we truly believe is not something we choose or fully control. If we are allowed to think freely and acquire knowledge without prejudice, we form conclusions based on what we believe to be correct, not necessarily on what we are told or what would be expedient. Our beliefs are the product of mental processes that are influenced by a multitude of factors and that go much deeper than conscious choice. In fact, if we consciously chose to believe in any god without sincerity and conviction, the belief would be a ruse. And of course if there were a god, he would certainly not be fooled by such pretense. Also, we would probably not feel very good about ourselves if we pretended to believe in something when we actually did not.

A Perfect Mess

If there is a god and he is omnipotent and good, why did he create a universe with so many imperfections? And I do not mean the imperfection of evil. That is discussed elsewhere. I mean the imperfections in the physical functioning of the universe. For example, we know that meteorites have hit the earth, and we think some have caused mass destruction. We know that large bodies have hit other planets and the moon, and we think worlds and even galaxies collide. We know that earthquakes, tornadoes, hurricanes, and other destructive forces often ravage the earth. We know that disease, birth defects, and accidents routinely maim and kill. Are these events evidence of an imperfect universe or natural phenomena that cannot be avoided? Or do they perhaps serve some higher purpose?

If these are natural phenomena that cannot be avoided, then the god who made them is not omnipotent, because he was unable to create a perfect universe, or he is unable to control it now that it is in place. If he were able to create and control with perfection but chose not to, then he is not altogether good, because his choice causes a lot of pain and suffering.

Another possibility is that he did create a perfect universe and is able to control it, and the imperfections we see serve some higher purpose that he intended. But if a god did create the imperfections we see for some higher purpose, that still shows a lack of omnipotence or goodness or both, because an omnipotent god who is good would create a universe to meet all of his purposes without the meteorites, earthquakes, or disease. It is not logical to think that such destructive events would be put in place by an omnipotent, benevolent god.

The Elusive Soul

The concept of the soul is related to the concept of God in that the soul is humankind's link to God for purposes of immortality. The concept is that every person has a soul, and when the body dies, the soul resides somewhere else until Judgment Day. At Judgment Day God picks the souls of the people he is pleased with and brings their bodies back to life to reside with him in heaven for eternity. Once the concept of god is accepted, the concepts of the soul, heaven, and immortality seem to follow.

But the soul is a hard concept to grasp. At least with the concept of god, we can imagine a human-like figure with great powers, but the soul is harder to imagine. By most accounts the soul contains no mass, is invisible, indivisible, and immortal, and it resides somewhere in the body but leaves the body upon death and resides somewhere else. Many philosophers have speculated on the soul. Some dismiss it as sheer fantasy, and some treat it as real and even offer details on its purpose, makeup, necessity, and other traits. Unfortunately, the soul, like many other religious concepts, cannot be proven and if accepted must be done so on faith.

Furthermore, the question arises as to exactly when the soul comes into existence. Is the soul created at conception, birth, or some other time? If the soul is created at conception, what happens if the fertilized egg fails to become an embryo? How will the egg exist in the hereafter? If eggs are fertilized in the laboratory or are cloned, do they have souls? If embryos are formed through artificial insemination, when does the soul come into existence?

If the soul is created sometime between conception and birth, how will an embryo or fetus that dies before birth exist in the hereafter? Will it exist as a partially developed human, or will its development be projected to some future state through divine intervention?

If the soul is created at birth, then fertilized eggs, embryos, and fetuses have no souls and therefore are not candidates for heaven.

In short, at what exact instant in the propagation of humans does the soul come into existence, and if the soul comes into existence before the human is fully developed, how will the undeveloped human exist in the hereafter?

And finally, in a much bigger picture, if humans are the only life-form that have souls, did God exist before humans evolved to the point of having souls? Since our soul is said to make us special compared to all other life-forms and indeed is our link with God, would the concept of god have any meaning if no souls existed? Fundamentalists don't have to grapple with this question since they believe that God created us in our present form, but for those who are religious and believe in evolution, the question exists: At exactly what stage in the evolutionary process did the soul come into being?

Can We Believe What We Read
The Bible is one of the primary sources of information about God. Yet the Bible contains some information that is questionable, controversial, contradictory, and vague. As said earlier, this is not an attempt to disparage the Bible, but since the Bible plays such an important role in the logic of believing in God, its credibility must be mentioned, at least from a broad perspective.

Most acknowledge that the Bible was written at different times by different people and has undergone multiple revisions. (The Quran is said to have been written over a shorter period from a single source and is said to remain in its original form.) Most agree that some parts of the Bible are more credible than others, yet all parts were written by mortals, often many years after the events that are described took place. With this in mind, I believe it is reasonable to surmise that one of the primary sources of information about God is subject to error.

Many of us have witnessed an event and then read or heard accounts of it later. Often what we read or heard was not consistent with what we witnessed. Even when accounts of an event are prepared by professional journalists shortly after the event took place, factual mistakes are often made. Similar comments can be made about witnesses in a court proceeding. Eyewitnesses to an event often differ on the details of the event they witnessed. Therefore, to assert that the Bible, or any lengthy, historical document written by many people over a period of time, is factual in every detail is not logical.

The intent is not to discredit the Bible, because almost certainly the Bible contains a lot of factual information. But it is impossible to know exactly what is factual and what is not. It is also impossible to know what information is religious and what is not. The common belief seems to be that whatever is in the Bible has religious implications, but we do not know that for sure. Those who wrote and revised the Bible may have included historical, biographical, descriptive, poetic, or other types of material that provided coherence or literary value but were not necessarily intended to have religious implications, and to draw religious conclusions from such material might give a meaning that was not intended.

Where Did the Wisdom Come From

If God is real, did he prepare the commandments and all the other guidance to live by based on his "specific system of beliefs"? If so, the guidance is arbitrary in that it is based on his individual judgment or preference as to what is good. If the guidance is based on some higher values or some absolute definition of what is good, then God is not omnipotent and is not the final authority. And even if the guidance is based on God's "specific system of beliefs" and those beliefs do represent an absolute definition of good, where did that absolute definition of good come from? Where did God get his wisdom?

This and many other questions related to God and other possible gods stem from trying to define a beginning. If there is a god, everything that followed him can be explained as coming from him. But where did he come from and what shaped his beliefs? A god without a beginning is not logical. Anything said to be infinitely old raises many questions of logic.

Where Did the Devil Come From
If the biblical God created the universe, where did the devil come from? It would not be logical for God to create the devil. Why would God create evil? And if the devil came about through some other means, then God is not omnipotent. He is not the sole creator.

Maybe God did create the devil, but maybe he did it for a holy reason. Maybe he did it to provide temptation to test believers. If so, he would have to give the devil free will. Without free will, the devil would just be part of the divine plan, and that would be no test. And he would have to give us free will too. If we did not have free will, the devil could not tempt us into doing something that was not in the divine plan. But if anyone other than God has free will, then God is not omnipotent. He is not in total control.

Role Model

> Reverend Right was a portly fellow
> And on Sundays he would bellow
> About all manner of sin
>
> But he just could not mention
> Gluttony, greed, or abstention
> Without a little grin

Let Us Get Personal

We are told that the Abrahamic god is a personal one, implying that he can be different things to different people. And since he is portrayed in so many different ways in the holy books, there is some logic to this assertion. He is portrayed as being both involved in humankind's activities and being passive; as being both an unknowable deity and a manlike one; as being both brutal and kind, vengeful and forgiving, warlike and peaceful. Although the portrayals point out inconsistencies, they do imply a god who can accommodate a wide variety of beliefs. The concept of a flexible god is good as far as making him personal or accessible to everyone; however, it is not so good as far as trying to define him. He would be so nebulous that few absolute statements or descriptions could be made about him.

God is also said to be personal in that he interacts with everyone at all times. Again, this is logical, given the nebulous god described above. If he is not a discrete entity, continual interaction with everyone can be imagined. He could be thought of as a kind of wave that spreads out over the universe or a beacon with individual rays going to each person in accordance with that person's needs or beliefs.

This concept of a personal god could be compared to pantheism. He is everywhere for everybody all the time. I do not think this is what the holy books intend, but there is a subtle, logical basis for such belief, and I delve much deeper into this concept later in the book.

What We Think

If there is a god and he is omnipotent, he can see inside our minds and know exactly what we are thinking at any time. He would know instantly if our thoughts were good or bad, pure or evil. He would know our needs, our vices, our sins, and our every intention. There would be no need for purposeful communications of any kind with such a god. There would be no need for prayers, confessions, sacrifices, rituals, and the like. In fact, many religious activities could be viewed as sacrilegious since they would imply that he was incapable of knowing what was in our minds otherwise.

I believe that if there is a god, he is omnipotent and knows our every inner feeling. If we said or did things that lacked sincerity or conviction, he would know. If we pretended to be pious, he would know. If we pretended to embrace him on Sunday and failed to be benevolent on Monday, he would know. In short, he would see reality without any filter or slant or pretense. I believe he would judge us based on that reality and nothing else, which means his judgment would be influenced more by our actions than by our stated beliefs, unless those stated beliefs were absolutely sincere. He would know.

Is God Good

If we accept the concept that there is a god, a fundamental question arises concerning his goodness. Is he good? We should follow him to the extent that he is good, and surely we would not want to follow a god who was not good. Yet we have no proof that any god is good. We have reason to believe that the Abrahamic god has done some good things, but we also have reason to believe that he is controlling, vengeful, needy, and even cruel. Any god-based beliefs are defendable only to the extent that the god is good.

An Agnostic's Path to God

An argument can be made that if an objective observer read the holy books, he would conclude that God is not altogether good. Would a god who is altogether good threaten people with an eternity of hell, would he use war as a means to achieve his goals, would he allow innocent babies to suffer and die, would he allow all the pain, suffering, misery, evil, and so forth, to exist? If he were omnipotent and good, he would find a way to avoid hell, suffering, and all the other bad things. That objective observer might just conclude that God is not altogether good, which brings into question the logic of unconditional devotion.

God and Hell

Logic indicates there is no reason to worry about hell. If there is a god and he is good, he would not commit us to eternal torture, regardless of what we did during our lifetimes. Such punishment is just not appropriate, especially when he has the power to change behavior. If there is a god and he is not good, our actions would not necessarily determine our fate. And if there is no god, the issue is moot.

Problems in Paradise

If there is a heaven and only certain people go there, some people in heaven would not have their mothers or fathers with them. If those in heaven remembered the parents left behind, they might feel great sorrow, and that would make heaven less than perfect. And since everyone has a mother and a father, there would be no way to hide the absence of either from those is heaven without distorting their reality. Unfortunately, such distortion would make heaven disingenuous.

The question also arises whether those in heaven will even know they are in heaven. If they do, as stated above, they might feel sorrow for those left behind. And if they do not know they are in heaven, they would have nothing to compare heaven to and therefore could not appreciate its grandeur. Also they would not realize that they were being rewarded for their life on earth.

It seems the only way heaven could be viewed as paradise or a reward would be to realize that you were there. And that would mean knowing that others you cared for were not. Maybe you would just be happy without knowing that you had a previous life on earth or that you had relationships on earth that were not continued in heaven. But either way would require that some or your memory be erased, which would change your perspective and make you into a different person.

Peer Pressure

> Before we ate
> Some wanted to pray

An Agnostic's Path to God

Not wanting to offend
Or maybe lacking courage
I bowed my head too
Afterward, I resented them
And me

Divine Design or Dice

One of the most heard arguments for the creation theory is that nothing as complex as the universe could have evolved by chance. Only design and creation by an omnipotent god could explain the complexities, the wonders, and the life we see today. The current name for this line of thinking is intelligent design.

This argument has at least two major flaws. First, it does not explain where the Abrahamic god or any other god came from. If there is a god and he is omnipotent, then certainly he could have created the universe in whatever form and by whatever method he wanted. But then the question becomes, where did he come from?

Second, it is not logical to think that something very complex could be designed but not evolved in stages over time. If the universe were created by design, then everything had to be known at the beginning. All knowledge about all things for all time had to exist at the time of creation. Whereas if the universe evolved, not everything had to be known at the beginning. Some simple beginning or basic start to get things going would be all that was needed, and then a more complex future could unfold.

Quantum theory holds that mass can materialize from nothing if certain conditions are met. Consider this happening on a large scale to put the basic building blocks of the universe in place. Then consider allowing enough time to pass so that natural forces shape the universe and cause it to become what we see today. These are not easy concepts to accept, but they are grounded in science and are no more far-fetched than the premise that an infinitely more complex reality was designed and created by an omnipotent god of unknown origin. In fact, it seems more logical to accept a simple beginning and an evolving complexity rather than a beginning requiring all the complexity at the very beginning.

Dragons in Utah

Direct statements, such as the earth is the third planet from the sun, or an elephant is bigger that a mouse, or the square root of nine is three, can be easily proved or disproved with observations, measurements, and calculations. But proving a negative statement is much harder. Take an outlandish statement such as this: There are no dragons in Utah. Most of us would agree that Utah is free of dragons. But how could you prove it with certainty? You might look all over Utah, but you could not look in every place at the same time. You could point out that there have been no reported sightings, but maybe the dragons are there and are just very good at hiding, or maybe some have been sighted and were not reported. You could allege that dragons are a fantasy and do not exist in reality, but that is not proof. That is a logical statement based on what we know, but it is not absolute proof.

The same quandary applies when discussing the logic of whether God exists. I may question his existence, I may offer logical statements in support of my doubts, and I may even point to the lack of objective, empirical evidence that he exists, but none of that is absolute proof. I cannot prove that God does not exist. And that is why I do not want to say I am an atheist. To be an atheist is to imply you know, and I believe knowing is impossible. And to me being an agnostic means you go where the logic or any compelling information takes you. And that is where I am.

God and the Eons

If there is a god and he is eternal, he is infinitely old. He always existed. He was not created. He did not come into existence at a specific time. He did not result from some event. In short, no matter how far back in time you go, he existed. This avoids the need to explain where he came from and what existed before him because an eternal god always existed, and nothing came before him. But the infinite age leads to other problems.

First, nothing we know of can last forever—not mass, not energy, not momentum, not anything. The second law of thermodynamics says that everything deteriorates, and no exception has ever been found. But of course an eternal god could be an exception because he is god.

But even if an eternal god is an exception, an infinite age causes problems of logic. An eternal god implies an immutable god. He never changes. Immutability is synonymous with eternal. But if there is a god, indications are he changed. If he created the universe, he changed. He reached a point in his existence when he wanted a universe. He existed for an infinitely long time and then for some reason decided he wanted a universe. That is change. Another change alluded to in the Bible concerns his involvement with humankind. The early parts of the Bible indicate that God was openly and directly involved with humankind, but in later parts he was not as directly involved. That is another change.

And if an eternal god is changeable, logic says he would produce an infinite number of outcomes. If he changed in one or two ways, in time he would change in other ways. It's logical. Anything that changes, anything that is not static, will produce all possible outcomes if given enough time.

A classic example makes this point very well: Suppose you had a monkey in a room with a typewriter, and all could survive forever. Given enough time, the monkey would move to the typewriter and push a key. It might take a year or a thousand years or more. But given enough time, a monkey in a room with a typewriter would push a key. Now, given a lot more time, the monkey would write a word. This could take millions of years because we assume the monkey is pushing the keys at random, and most of what is typed would be gibberish. But it would eventually happen. At some point, the monkey would write a word. And by extension, given much, much more time, the monkey would write a sentence, a paragraph, and yes, even a book. And although it stretches the mind to imagine enough time, if time were unlimited, if time were infinite, the monkey would eventually write the complete works of Shakespeare and more.

The point is that given enough time, an omnipotent god who is subject to change will produce all possible outcomes. He has the time, he has the power, and he has demonstrated change. Those parameters will inevitably lead to an infinite number of outcomes. There is no law that says god has to change in the future, but given the past, we cannot be sure.

God's Home away from Home

If a god created the universe, he had to reside somewhere else before the creation. He could not have resided in a nonexistent universe. He may still reside somewhere else, for all we know, but he had to reside somewhere other than the universe before he created it. Therefore, when we speak of the universe he created, we are not including the place where he came from, unless he included that place as part of the universe when he created it.

But the question this leads to is, where did this god come from? We know he came from somewhere other than the universe he created, but we do not know how to think about that. How big is the place he came from? What else was there? Does he still reside there, or does he now reside in the universe? Was the place he came from included in the universe he created? If so, what happened to it, and what part of the universe is it now in?

Maybe there was nothing before the universe, except the spirit or essence of god, and the material god, if one exists, was created along with everything else. That would help resolve the question of the creator god's whereabouts before the creation, but it raises the question of where the spirit came from. And if this god's spirit existed, were there other spirits too, and if so, did any of them create anything? It is a nebulous subject at best, but I believe any scenario involving a god's presence before the universe existed raises problems of logic.

Telewhat
Some scientific concepts would challenge religious beliefs if the concepts became reality. One such concept is teleportation.

An Agnostic's Path to God

Many religious people believe that we are more than our physical makeup. They believe we have a soul, which makes us different from other animals and provides our link with God. Someday it may be possible to teleport matter, and that could determine if we are more than our physical makeup.

Scientists may be able to transfer matter from one location to another by disassembling it into elementary particles at one location and reassembling them at another, or by describing the type, relationship, and other attributes of all the elementary particles in a piece of matter at one location and constructing an identical piece at another. This is beyond present-day capabilities, although it has been reported that single elementary particles have already been teleported. But the point is that some day it may be possible to teleport people, and if we could teleport people, we would just be transferring the physical matter. It would not be possible to transfer something with no mass, like the soul. Therefore, the person transferred would be identical in all physical respects to the original, but would be without any nonphysical constituents. Then, we would have to wonder if that person was any different from the original. And the religious question would be the following: Would a teleported person have his or her soul stripped away, making that person ineligible for heaven?

God in the Gaps

Just because there are gaps in our knowledge does not mean there is a god. We may never have a complete understanding of all physical phenomena, but it is a little disingenuous to use our ignorance as evidence that there is a god. Our knowledge is continuously expanding. I think most will agree that we know more today than we did a year ago or a hundred years ago or a thousand years ago. And I think if we stay around, we will continually learn more. The present gaps in our knowledge will close, and new ones will likely open, but those gaps will not prove anything of a religious or supernatural nature. To allege otherwise is an illogical way of trying to justify a belief in god.

In the distant past, the use of supernatural explanations was common. But as knowledge increased, we relied less on supernatural explanations and more on proven facts, empirical data, experimentation, and so forth, for explanations. But some people point to things we still cannot explain or prove and say that God is the answer. Logic tells me that if there is a god, proof of his existence will come from what we know, not from what we do not know.

No Pain, No Gain

As discussed elsewhere, one reason some people do not believe in God is because of all the pain, suffering, and evil that exist in the world. They feel that if there were a god and he was good and omnipotent, he would not allow such pain, suffering, and evil to exist. However, I have heard others attempt to justify the pain and suffering by saying that it is necessary to make us fully appreciate the other parts of life. They say that God allows the bad to exist to make us fully appreciate the good. There is some merit to this thinking in that if we feel pain or suffer in some way or are the victims of evil, we feel better when the pain or suffering or evil stops.

However, there are flaws to this logic. First, those who died as a result of the evil are gone. They do not rejoice when it stops. Second, most of those who suffer in horrendous ways do not forget the suffering, even when it ends. Third, those who lost family or friends are not easily comforted by knowing that the pain, suffering, evil, and so forth, has stopped. Fourth, and most important, concerns God's role.

If there is a god and he is good and omnipotent, he would find a way to make us appreciate life to the fullest without the need for pain and suffering. If he could not do this, he would not be omnipotent. It is illogical to try to justify the coexistence of a good and omnipotent god with pain, suffering, and evil. A god that allows such is either not good, or not omnipotent, or neither.

Religion and Morality

Some say we must have religion to have morality. The argument is that even if we do not believe in God, we must accept that our morality or sense of right and wrong stems from him.

Logic, history, observations, experience, and even religious practices tell me this is not true.

The Bible contains some sound moral guidance. But it also contains descriptions of God's involvement in infanticide, genocide, punishing of innocents, damning of future generations, animal sacrifices, and suffering of all kinds, as well as God's controlling, heavy-handed, vindictive, and jealous behavior. Certainly, some of the commandments, the golden rule, some of the teachings of Jesus and other religious figures, and indeed, many parts of the Bible and the Quran, contain great words to live by. But God and Jesus also accepted and promoted slavery and allowed women to be treated as second-class citizens. Not until the last hundred-plus years have we seen slavery abolished and women empowered in some parts of the world. So if morality comes from God or religion, how come the slaves were freed and women were empowered? Neither change came from God or religion. Both came from the goodness of humans. And I believe most everyone would have to agree that efforts to provide equal rights and treatment to gays did not stem from God or religion. Whether we agree with such efforts or not, we have to concede that such efforts were made in spite of religion rather than because of it.

Logic indicates that religion is not a prerequisite of morality. Religion contains many moral lessons, but it contains many immoral ones too. Certainly many religious people are moral, but many non-religious people are moral too. There is just no compelling argument that a person must be religious to be moral or that religion in general is a prerequisite to morality.

Indeed, good behavior is abundant in many societies, both now and historically, that are devoid of the Abrahamic god. And high standards of morality are routinely practiced by atheists, agnostics, secularists, and others who are opposed to, uninterested in, or ambivalent toward religion. As I have said before, I am a nonbeliever in large part because of the way God is depicted in the holy books. The Abrahamic god is not a prerequisite to morality. Indeed, considering his behavior as described in the holy books, a stronger argument could be made that he is a hindrance.

The Fine-Tuning Argument

This argument is similar to the intelligent design argument, except instead of asserting that our universe could not be the way it is without a divine designer, the fine-tuning argument asserts that there is a fine-tuner. The argument is that since certain physical parameters have to be very close to the way we find them for the universe to be the way it is and support life as we know it, this could only have come about through divine intervention.

No one denies that our universe would be very different if the speed of light, the mass of elementary particles, the strength of the basic forces, the number of space dimensions we experience, the rate the universe expanded, and so forth, were not almost exactly as we find them; however, this apparent fine-tuning is not necessarily proof of a supreme being. Consider the following:

The fine-tuning argument focuses on existing life. To argue that certain conditions had to be very finely tuned to allow for the possibility of such life ignores the billions of years of evolution to get to where we are based on natural selection, which of course factored in the conditions that existed during the selection process. Actually, if you take the end results of many occurrences, processes, or systems and say that they would not have turned out the exact same way if past events had not been finely tuned, that does not mean that only through divine intervention could those specific results have occurred. It just means that the past events produced certain outcomes. Different events would have produced different outcomes. Consider a baseball game, a person's life, or a weather system: For any given outcome, or indeed any given instant, to be a certain way, events leading up to that outcome or instant had to be a certain way. That is not divine intervention. That is just reality. In the case of the universe, different physical circumstances could have produced different universes and life-forms that we cannot imagine. There is nothing that requires the universe be exactly as we know it. And the life-forms we know did not have to be exactly as they are. The universe and life-forms we are familiar with are simply the result of the reality that occurred.

Second, if the universe is fine-tuned for life, why are most places in the universe hostile to life? As far as we can tell, the surface of the earth is the only place that could support higher life-forms, and honestly, only a small fraction of that area is habitable by humans. It is possible that other locations will be discovered in the universe where people could survive without major life support systems, but still, when the entire universe is considered, only a very tiny fraction is habitable. That is not exactly fine-tuning.

Third, fine-tuning is an illogical argument for those who believe in an omnipotent god, because such a god could have made life that could live in a variety of conditions. Fine-tuning of environmental factors is only a concept that applies if we limit our thinking to life as we know it. An omnipotent god could have created life in many different forms to survive in many different conditions.

And we have to consider that if there were a god and he created the universe, he would have to be more finely tuned and evolved than the universe he created. So, for the argument that the universe is too finely tuned to have evolved naturally, we have to accept that an entity far more finely tuned had to exist before the universe was created. And of course that begs the question of where that entity came from. If you say that

that entity is God and had no beginning because he is eternal, you could make the same argument about the universe. Maybe it, or some version of it, was always here. But even if the universe is not eternal and did start at some specific time in the past, as most scientists think, that does not necessarily mean there was divine intervention. It could mean that the universe started in some natural way (big bang) that we can imagine and describe but do not fully understand.

And I have to mention inflation theory when talking about fine-tuning. Inflation theory is the premise that our universe underwent tremendous expansion for a brief period very early in its formation, and although only a theory, it does have scientific merit, according to many cosmologists. It has merit because it explains a lot of what we know about the universe, such as the flatness of space, the uniformity of the universe we see, cosmic acceleration, and even details about the mechanism of the big bang. But along with the theory comes the likelihood that the inflation or expansion did not stop in other locations that we cannot see, forming multiple and perhaps an infinite number of other universes, only some of which would be supportive of life as we know it. This multiverse scenario renders moot the "fine-tuning" debate about our universe, because if there are many, perhaps an infinite number of universes, naturally we would be in one that favored us. It is kind of like our position on earth as opposed to Venus or Saturn or some planet light years away. (Many physicists posit the formation of parallel universes to explain quantum weirdness too; however, I will not delve into that because inflation theory gives us plenty of universes to work with:)

Inflation theory and its accompanying multiverse speculation are admittedly far-fetched and unprovable at present, and therefore they do not make a strong argument. But I mention it because it is rooted in sound cosmology, it is consistent with a lot of what we know, and it is also consistent with how we have thought in the past. At one time we thought the earth was all there was, except for a few lights in the sky. Then we thought the same about our solar system and even our galaxy. Now we know there are untold numbers of galaxies out there, and each likely contains many solar systems. It is not inconsistent or inconceivable to think that there are vast numbers of universes out there too.

I do not want to be too insensitive to those who make the fine-tuning or intelligent design arguments, but both are just different ways of saying God created the universe. I think it is more genuine to just say God created the universe, if that is what you believe, rather than inventing a pseudoscientific way of saying it. There are irreconcilable differences between religion and science, and if we try to make them seem compatible or try too hard to use science to make religious arguments, we run the risk of being apologetic to the point of being ridiculous.

Two

Religion 1

In the next two chapters, I try to identify some of the most problematic areas associated with religion. I made two chapters because one chapter would be too long. As with other parts of the book, I try to make my point without being mean-spirited, disingenuous, or petty. The literature is full of such religious criticism, and much of it is slanted to the point of diminishing the credibility of the writer and what is said. I try to avoid that. Whenever I can, I use logic as the basis of my arguments, and even if you do not agree with what I say, I hope you will believe that I try to avoid prejudicial rhetoric that irritates more than informs.

What Keeps Us Apart

Race, color, national origin, gender, age, and religion are basic differences among us that can cause divisiveness. In the

An Agnostic's Path to God

United States, we have laws against discriminating on the basis of these differences, but of course, the differences still keep us apart to some extent, as they do throughout the world. We have a choice in only one of these basic differences: religion. I am not necessarily saying that we choose our religion, because many people are taught a religion from birth or are otherwise predisposed toward a certain religion without much choice. I am just saying that religion is the only basic difference among us for which there is even the possibility of choice.

Logic indicates that if we could eliminate even one of our differences, we could all get along better. Of course it is not possible to eliminate religious differences, because that would mean doing away with religion. But logic suggests that the world would be better off without religion. Some might argue that religion helps us by teaching forgiveness, benevolence, love, and other good things. Others might argue that religion hurts us by fostering hatred, terrorism, wars, and other bad things. Certainly some good comes from religion. To argue otherwise would be disingenuous. But with equal certainty, religion causes divisiveness among the people of the world and thereby contributes to much hatred, pain, suffering, and other bad things. Past wars, crusades, witch-hunts, ethnic cleansing programs, jihads, and the Inquisition, among other atrocities, exemplify the divisiveness. Our present-day situation shows it continues.

I believe even those who embrace religion with passion and conviction would agree that religious differences keep us apart.

What about Jesus, Muhammad, and Others

Jesus, Muhammad, and other religious leaders associated with God, and even religious leaders not associated with God, such as Buddha, Confucius, and Lao-tzu, were very influential men. They have had a profound influence on humanity. But were they prophets, messiahs, or gods, or were they just mortal men of great charisma, character, and wisdom? If Jesus rose from the dead as Christians believe, that would be compelling evidence that he was something other than human. But that assertion is one of the most disputed and debated issues in all of religion. In fact, we just don't know for certain whether God or a personification of God or even a prophet of God has ever walked among us. Many religious leaders of the past were very wise and passed along much inspiration, wisdom, and guidance, but logic tells me they were all human.

If an omnipotent being had ever walked this earth, logic tells me that there would be indisputable, compelling evidence of his presence, especially if he had been our creator and wanted to speak to us through his actions. Would the creator of the universe walk among us, or send someone to walk among us, and not make sure that his presence was documented beyond all doubt? It does not seem logical that he would allow doubt to exist about such an important event, especially if he was our creator and held our eternal future in his hands. He would recognize the importance of clear understanding and would make sure that all future generations knew of his visit and his intentions; otherwise, he would be denying all who could not accept him on faith the ability to embrace his greatness, learn from his teachings, and benefit from his rewards.

No Hell for Me

>I am not too religious
>You can probably tell
>But that does not mean
>I am going to hell
>
>Because if there is a god
>And he is great and good
>He will accept some blame
>For being misunderstood

Who Is in Charge

Buddhists do not embrace a god or supreme being. They seek wisdom, guidance, and comfort from within. Instead of relying on a supreme being for answers, they rely on a process of looking within themselves for enlightenment. No one can say whether theism or nontheism is correct or indeed if one is better than the other, but comparing the two helps us recognize that belief systems vary greatly.

Christians, Muslims, Jews, and other followers of god-based religions look to a higher force than humankind to explain where we came from, how we should live our lives, and where we are going. They feel their beliefs are justified, and they find comfort in believing as they do. And their beliefs absolve them from seeking answers beyond their god and allow them to place their fate in the hands of their god.

Buddhists and others who do not accept a higher force must seek answers on their own, and looking within through meditation is a common way of doing this. Having faith in your mind and in your ability to find enlightenment with your own mind seems more logical to me than having faith in a supreme being. Both paths rely to some extent on faith, but the nontheistic path allows you to find answers that do not violate your logic. I am not necessarily trying to defend or promote Buddhism or any other nontheistic belief system, but I am suggesting that belief systems devoid of illogical thinking reflect reality better than do those based on the supernatural.

Why Apologize

Some theologians and apologists often propose ways the supernatural events described in the holy books could have occurred without divine intervention. They propose ways the events could have occurred without violating accepted laws of nature. I do not understand this. An omnipotent god could do anything mentioned in the Bible or the Quran and much more. Parting the sea, turning people to salt, raising the dead, healing the sick, turning water to wine, putting thoughts into people's heads—all would be no challenge to the creator of the universe. I question the logic of trying to explain such events in terms of natural phenomena. It seems to me the apologists should let their god be omnipotent and quit trying to make religion and reality compatible. If you accept God, then you accept some supernatural occurrences, and there is no need to conjure up excuses.

What Are the Odds

Christians, Muslims, and Jews believe in the Abrahamic god; however, the three religions have fundamental differences that can make them incompatible. Indeed, some in one religion may view those in another as having no chance of going to heaven. And each of the three has one or more subgroups that can be incompatible too. Christianity includes the Roman Catholic Church, the Eastern Orthodox Church, and many Protestant churches. The major subsets in Islam are the Shiites and the Sunnis, and the Shiites are split into various sects. Judaism has multiple sects too, spanning the spectrum from the very liberal to the ultraconservative. In short, those who identify with the Abrahamic god have many different beliefs, and they cannot all be right.

If we apply cold, hard reasoning to the question of going to heaven, we might come up with something like this: First, assume that the Abrahamic god is real, and at least some of his followers will go to heaven. Second, count up all the Christians, Muslims, and Jews in the world. Third, divide them into groups with incompatible beliefs. Fourth, take the largest group and assume those are the ones who will be favored by God. And fifth, consider that some members of the favored group may not be selected because of their transgressions. Therefore, of all who embrace the Abrahamic god, only those from the favored group who meet the selection criteria will be heaven bound. (I know this analysis is not precise because there may be overlap of groups and other factors to consider, but my point is that the incompatible beliefs of those who embrace the Abrahamic god may exclude many of them from heaven.)

There are billions of good people in the world who are not Christian, Muslim, or Jewish and could be candidates for heaven if good behavior and deeds were considered, so it is possible some of them will end up in heaven. I know some religious groups believe that you must have faith in god to even have a chance at heaven, and if one of those groups ends up being right, only the faithful will go to heaven. But other religious groups put more credence in how you live than in what you believe, and if one of them ends up being right, there could be many people in heaven who are not Christians, Muslims, or Jews.

Some Christians, Muslims, and Jews may assert that the above comments are illogical. They may say that you cannot combine their group or subgroup with all the others when considering the odds of going to heaven. They may argue that other religious groups are wrong, and the members will not go to heaven, but they may assert that they are sure they are right, and many of their members will indeed go to heaven. They have a valid point. If their beliefs turn out to be the ones favored by God, then it is not fair to lump them with the others. But we will not know if any group is favored until Judgment Day, and even if there is such a day, it may not be clear which, if any, group is favored.

Regardless, I believe it is logical to believe that if there is an Abrahamic god, and if he picks some people to go to heaven, the odds for Christians, Muslims, and Jews going may be no better than the odds for others.

A Little Prayer

> If you are there
> Please protect us
> From those who do evil
> In your name
> Amen

What Is the Difference

I know some people who are very religious. They sincerely believe in God and they are not hypocrites. They try to live their lives in a devout way. However, none of them is perfect. One managed his mother's assets such that she could get public assistance without first having to spend her own money, thus leaving more money for him when she died. Another complains a lot. Another routinely does personal business while on her employer's payroll. Another overeats to the point of being obese. The list could go on and on.

Such criticism does not diminish the credibility of any religion, and I know it is petty and unfair to criticize religion simply because religious people are less than perfect. But the criticism was stated to lead into the question: What is the difference between a religious person and one who is not? All people have faults. All people sin. And the sins, even of religious people, vary from the minor ones mentioned above to horrendous ones, such as multiple murders committed by a religious fanatic or an insane mother killing her children to prove her faith in God. (Was Abraham insane?)

It seems to me the difference between a religious person and a nonreligious person is in the mind. It is a personal belief that has no effect beyond the mind. A religious person has religious beliefs, and a nonreligious person does not. I do not think the difference between the two typically has anything to do with right or wrong, with values or goodness, or with a destiny. I think it has to do with what a person believes and nothing more. Embracing a certain belief system makes some people feel better, and while that is not necessarily wrong, it is not logical to think that a mind-set can affect the physical world or lead to life after death.

The Big Mo

Collectively, the world's great religions expend a lot of effort on self-promotion. Through preaching, missionary work, publications, funding, lobbying, coercion, fear, and so on, they promote their dogma and resist challenges to it. In many places organized religion has been extremely successful in penetrating governments, influencing societies, recruiting followers, and inducing believers to give money, time, energy, and even their lives to the furtherance of the belief.

Collectively, billions of people embrace Judaism, Christianity, and Islam. And when this many people have a personal, vested interest in a belief system, the system has momentum. The system is promoted, touted, perpetuated, and defended based in large part on momentum, self-serving dogma, and emotion. Objectivity goes out the window. Generation after generation of families are raised on the dogma. The dogma becomes more entrenched. Debate is limited. Objective and critical self-evaluation are rare. The dogma is paramount. Bureaucratic thinking takes hold. Old leaders are in control. Fresh thinking is resisted. Change is resisted. The momentum carries the juggernaut along, right or wrong, good or bad, day after day. The system is self-perpetuating. We can no longer judge it based on its merits. Many even forget its merits. It is just there. We cannot avoid it. We cannot control it. It can become evil. It can make the world a dark place. It can corrupt us. It can deceive us. It can divide us. It can kill us.

A Mind Is a Terrible Thing to Waste
One of the biggest drawbacks to organized religion is how it impedes thinking. People are taught to accept the religious teachings without question. They are even made to feel guilty if they do ask questions or feel doubt. Their thinking becomes programmed and unable to venture outside the narrow path endorsed by the religious doctrine. They accept it as fact and do not question the logic. Their religious beliefs get so entrenched and become such a part of their lives that they resent anyone who questions them or anything that is not consistent with their way of looking at things.

Such narrow-mindedness perpetuates itself by inhibiting open discussions and objective thinking. I believe this barrier to original and creative thinking makes organized religion harmful in some ways. I have always felt that knowledge is the key to solving our problems, and anything that inhibits the objective and open exploration and exchange of ideas is a deterrent to gaining such knowledge.

An Agnostic's Path to God

The Big Promise

Perhaps the most daunting thing any of us can face is death with no hope of anything beyond, and I believe it is this fear that motivates many people toward religion. It is hard for anyone to contemplate an absolute, irreversible end. One second there is life, and the next there is nothing and never will be again. The finality of death makes life seem frivolous, fragile, ephemeral. The thought of eternal nothingness scares us. We like to think that our existence has some long-term meaning. We like to think that we will leave some mark that will last forever. And the thought that nothing will survive the passage of time is hard to accept.

Of course some things we do can last beyond our death. Our children can pass along our genes, and our acquaintances can harbor memories of us. Fame, fortune, great accomplishments, and so forth, can leave a mark, but none will last. Even if we do something so astounding that it changes the world, eventually history fades, facts get distorted, and issues become moot. Consider a thousand years from now, a million, a billion. Consider when the sun burns out, and our solar system disappears. What significance will our existence have then? Consider when the universe expands and cools or contracts and explodes or follows through on whatever its fate will be. Will our time on earth have any meaning then? Nothing is static. Nothing can survive the test of time. Nothing will last forever. But religion promises otherwise.

And religion's promise of immortality ensures its survival. How enticing to embrace a belief that promises eternal life. How attractive to follow a dogma that promises life after death. Even if the beliefs are not altogether factual or provable or logical, the promise is wonderful. Many accept a reality based on the supernatural because of the promise of immortality. Many live in accordance with religious teachings because of the promise. Many even give their life in the name of religion because of the promise. Think about this: How many would believe in a supreme being without the promise of life after death? How many faithful practitioners would we see; indeed, how many martyrs would there be without the promise of eternal life? In short, are we religious because of some irresistible, undeniable truth that we cannot ignore, or are we religious because we want to come back to life after we die?

A Constant Wonder
There is little information in the Bible or the Quran about the physical universe beyond some generalities, fabrications, fables, or superficial information. Certainly if there is a god and he created the universe, he would have a complete understanding of all the physical aspects of it. Think how compelling the holy books would be if they contained some physical constants or facts that were not known at the time they were written. Think how far that would go to prove God's existence and omnipotence to future generations.

There are many physical facts about the universe that could easily be passed along. The number pi comes to mind, which is the ratio of the circumference of a circle to its diameter. Take any circle in a flat plane, divide its circumference by its diameter, and you get the number pi. The speed of light in a vacuum is another well-defined constant. Or how about the relationship between the atomic masses of hydrogen and helium or between any two elements, for that matter? Any of these constants could have been passed along in ways that would be universally understandable. And think how astounding it would have been if, when we discovered pi or learned to measure the speed of light or the masses of elements, those facts could have been clearly related to information in the Bible or the Quran.

God could have provided simple, straightforward information to demonstrate the credibility of what many believe to be the most important documents ever written. Of course, the lack of such information does not necessarily mean the holy books are wrong on other accounts. But if the Bible or the Quran contained physical facts that transcended what was knowable by humans at the time they were written, their credibility on all accounts would be greatly enhanced.

Women and Children
The Abrahamic religions are patriarchal and sexist toward women, and some exploit children. Without going into a lot of detail

regarding the treatment of women, I will just pose a few questions: Is God referred to as a man or a woman? Did God choose men or women to lead his chosen people? How many of the prophets were women? How many of the apostles or disciples were women? How many books of the Bible or the Quran are credited to women? How many religious leaders have been women? How many popes have been women? Are women throughout the religious world generally treated equal to men?

Also, some religions exploit women by allowing polygamy, denying women educational opportunities, barring women from positions of leadership, forbidding birth control and divorce, and generally treating women as second-class citizens. And remember, Lot offered to sacrifice his two virgin daughters to save his male visitors.

Some religions exploit children by allowing pedophilia, enticing children to perform acts of violence, and using them for free labor.

Cherry-Picking for the Bible

The Bible is made up of a collection of documents that were written and gathered over hundreds of years. The documents were written by many different people and edited and revised by many others. Many other documents were reviewed for inclusion but were deemed unsuitable. In short, the Bible was not cast in stone from the beginning as the

Ten Commandments supposedly were, but instead it came together and evolved over centuries to its present form. A lot of subjective decisions were made over the years as to what to include in the Bible and what to exclude.

Many Christians and Jews point to the Bible or parts of it as a basis for their religious belief, and they view the Bible as the word of God or the absolute truth. They do not think about it being written and edited by humans. They do not think about it in terms of having a lot of documents to pick from and picking only those that support or promote a certain theme or belief. Other gospels, historical documents, miracle stories, creation myths, and the like, were available when the Bible was being developed but were not included for specific reasons. In short, the Bible is a creation of humans, not only in what it contains, but also in what it does not.

Terrorism 101
Religious differences can lead to prejudices, discrimination, hate, violence, and even terrorism. A manifestation of religious evil is when people are willing to kill themselves and others in the name of religion.

Jewish Claim to Israel
The world was sympathetic with the Jews following the Holocaust, and when they wanted to occupy their so-called

biblical homeland, there was a lot of support. Of course the support did not come from the Palestinians who were displaced or the Arab world in general. The intent here is not to debate the Israel/Palestine issue, but to point out that the Jewish claim to the area is based on the Bible. I too am sympathetic with the Jews, but I must confess I see the Arab side as well.

Consider if a group staked a claim to Vermont and used an ancient religious document as the basis of its claim. There could be some merit to this metaphor because there were Native Americans in Vermont before the Europeans came. Consider if the group went to the world bodies and obtained support for their claim, especially from a group of rich, powerful nations that pledged financial and military aid. And finally, suppose the group bought a lot of land in Vermont and declared its independence from the existing government and was then recognized by most of the world as a sovereign nation. Would the displaced residents of Vermont and even the rest of the United States feel good about that?

Morality or Obedience
Are those who make ethical judgments based on religious convictions good, or are they just being religious? When a person follows the ethics of an accepted religious practice, that person is not necessarily making decisions based on personal beliefs but could simply be following his or her religious

teachings. This raises the following question: Are the decisions being made out of a desire to do the right thing or out of a fear of being punished for going against religious doctrine?

Certainly the guidance of "thou shalt not kill" has merit, but following it for religious reasons does not necessarily mean a person is against killing. It could mean that the person does not want to go against the teachings of his god. In contrast, a nonreligious person who believes "thou shalt not kill" is simply against killing. That person has no religious motivation to avoid killing. Nonreligious people make ethical judgments based on something other than religious teachings.

I do not mean to imply that religious people are robots who act without thought. And I know that religious teachings can influence nonreligious people too. But I think it is fair to say that moral decisions by religious people are not necessarily a result of their personal values. Their moral decisions could be a result of their desire to follow their religious teachings.

The Meat of the Matter

Neither Christians, Muslims, nor Jews prohibit the eating of meat. Some have rules regarding when meat can be eaten, what kinds of meat are acceptable, or how the meat should be prepared, but all allow the eating of animals. This contribution to the mistreatment of animals is inconsistent with religious teachings of benevolence. If we accept that animals feel pain, then we must accept that we contribute to their pain by eating them. And if we accept that animals have a consciousness, we must accept that we relegate many of them to a life of misery when we eat them. Of course many people eat meat without thinking about the effects of their action on the animals, but their lack of sensitivity does not diminish the plight of the animals.

Some may point to the holy books to justify the eating of animals. But such teachings are dated. The days when animals had a natural life until they were killed and eaten have long passed. Even in those days, there was cruelty involved, but at least the animals had some quality of life before they were killed. It is not like that today. Today most animals we eat are raised in very controlled, confined settings and do not experience a natural life before they are killed. They are born, raised, and slaughtered in industrial operations without regard for their dignity, consciousness, or feelings. They never see the sunshine or feel the rain. Some exist in small cages and are unable to even walk around. They are confined in an artificial, controlled environment until they are ready for slaughter. Many have been bred strictly for optimum meat production, which has made them very fragile in other ways. Many are routinely given antibiotics to fight infections that can be rampant in their confined environment, and many are fed hormones to stimulate growth. We cannot be righteous, benevolent, or altogether good when we contribute to such operations. With every bite of meat we eat, we contribute to the inhumane treatment of animals, not to mention that we swallow a myriad of unnatural chemicals that could damage our health.

Buddhists are taught to respect all life-forms and therefore do not eat animals. It seems to me that the Christians, Muslims, and Jews could learn from this benevolent philosophy.

I personally quit eating animals many years ago after seeing firsthand how they were managed in concentrated animal-feeding operations. I was raised on a small farm and knew that most farm animals ended up being eaten, but at least they had a somewhat natural life until they were slaughtered. That is just not true anymore. Most animals that we eat today have nothing resembling a natural life. I believe if more people visited the places where animals are grown, killed, and processed, we would have more vegetarians. And I believe we would be healthier and happier as a result.

The Second Creation

It appears the holy books were not created along with everything else; that is, God created everything and then some time later communicated with the prophets to create the holy books. If God did create the universe and then later created the holy books, this amounts to a second creation and shows that the first creation is not a one-time event, which opens the door to the possibility of further creations in the future.

Or maybe the holy books contain messages from God that were in his mind from the beginning and were simply communicated at a later time. This softens the second creation dilemma, but if the words were simply revealed to or passed through the prophets, did they have free will when passing his messages along? If so, we do not know if the messages were God's or the prophets'. Maybe the prophets did not have free will when conveying God's messages, but how do we know that? They were humans, and all their writings show signs of human influence.

Further, since the prophets were of different nationalities and spoke different languages, communications with them had to be in different languages. Of course God could easily be multilingual, but to attribute human language skills to God personifies him to some extent. Maybe God did not use language to communicate with the prophets. Maybe he put the messages in their minds through telepathy or some other nonverbal way. But then the prophets would have had to put the messages in words themselves to pass along to the world, and converting thoughts to words can lead to unintended meanings.

To add even more uncertainty regarding the words of the prophets, some scholars believe that the words were not even intended as prophecies but rather were historical accounts or descriptions of conditions at the time. The language was made metaphorical in hopes of avoiding persecution from the authorities. Therefore, we may be conjuring up prophecies where none were intended. We just do not know.

In summary, we cannot be sure the messages from the prophets came entirely from God, and we are not even sure if they were meant to be prophecies. When God speaks to us through human prophets, we have to take the prophet's word for the accuracy of the message. And to assert that the messages are completely accurate is to assert that the prophets were perfect as to motive and accuracy. And remember, those who compiled the holy books, especially the Bible, had multiple writings claiming to be prophecies to pick from. Therefore, the final product is questionable as to source, intent, and selection. It is just not logical to assume that everything in the holy books is the unaltered word of God.

No Clear Winner

Much of the pain, suffering, misery, and evil that has occurred throughout history and continues today is the result of religious differences. Religion can bring out the best in people, but religious differences can bring out the worst. This does not make religion bad, nor does it make the believers wrong. But it does bring into question the benefit of religion in general. Religion has brought comfort to many millions of people, but certainly is has brought misery, pain, and death to millions as well. If the overall worth of a thing is to be judged by the cumulative good or bad associated with that thing, organized religion would be no clear winner.

Come Judgment Day

The basis for determining who will go to heaven on Judgment Day is not real clear. Both the Bible and the Quran talk of faith and deeds as being important. Consequently, some religious people believe faith is paramount, while others believe deeds are. Since we have more control over our deeds than our faith, I hope deeds win the day. Also, there are many good, moral people in the world who may lack faith because they are ignorant of the Abrahamic god.

It is easy to see why some put more emphasis on belief and faith than on conduct and character. The Ten Commandments, the most famous of God's edicts, deal first with worshiping, then with behavior. The message seems to be that faith in God is more important than leading a moral life.

But logic makes me think that if there is a god, he would value conduct over anything else. A god who says you could live an exemplary life as far as moral conduct is concerned, but you could end up in hell if you lack an uncontrollable emotion or are unaware of him, is not a benevolent god who loves humankind.

The Power of Dogma

> They wanted a baby, so they prayed to God
> When the baby was born, they thanked God
> As she grew, they said they were blessed by God
> When she laughed, they said God was good
> When she got sick, they said it is God's will
> When she got worse, they said she is in God's hands
> When she died, they said God had spoken
> Then they said she was in heaven with God

Self-Serving

The self-serving practices of many religions often cause pain, suffering, and confusion. One such practice is the threat of hell. When religious leaders threaten patrons with hell to gain obedience, they cause fear and confusion, especially among the children. Many of us who were exposed to religion at a young age, especially the religions that rely on threats of hell to keep patrons in line, remember well the descriptions of agonizing and everlasting hell.

Another such practice is missionary work. Christian missionaries have gone to places where the indigenous people were happy and well adjusted and had belief systems that predated Christianity. Yet the missionaries would belittle the indigenous beliefs and try to convert the natives to Christianity. This often caused confusion and loss of identity. I know many

Christians feel obligated to proselytize, but the practice is selfish and harmful in many instances.

Another such practice is the condemnation of birth control. This act alone probably contributes more to human suffering than all natural disasters combined. Millions of babies a year are born into poverty, suffering, and squalor because their parents fear that family planning is a sin.

Religious teachings that contribute to the suffering of humankind are questionable, and such teachings whose underlying goal is simply to promote the religion may be evil.

Judge Not

One of the most hateful comments I have ever heard came after some county sheriffs in my home state of Missouri put "In God We Trust" bumper stickers on the backs of their patrol cars. When some people criticized the move, citing the need for separation of church and state, a woman in support of the stickers said, "Wouldn't you love to be around those people when they are dying and hear them ask God for help?" I have thought about that comment many times, and I believe it is a vengeful, judgmental, hateful statement.

Alas, this woman's comment sounds all too familiar. While most religious people I have known would get no joy from someone else's pain, a few do speak in judgmental or vengeful terms. They say in essence that if you do not accept their god on their terms, you will suffer later, and they will enjoy knowing that you suffer. Some will speak as this woman did, some will say how they pity you, and some will say they will pray for you, statements that all seek to demean you for not believing as they do.

Certainly, the holy books portray a judgmental, vengeful God, but he did make it clear that judgment and vengeance should be left to him. Therefore, we mortals should not judge the actions of others or talk in vengeful terms. Honestly, I doubt if the woman would get any joy from hearing a dying skeptic ask God for help, but it is demeaning to her and her religion to say such things.

How We See Things

One of the truest and most profound statements I have ever heard is the following: *"We don't see things as they are. We see things as we are."* This statement explains a lot of things about religion, science, art, history, people, and indeed everything we think we know. It explains why cultures clash, why passions differ, why objectivity is rare, why "facts" conflict, why religious differences divide us in harmful ways. If you could pick only one statement in an attempt to explain why we are the way we are, I believe this would be the one.

Gary L. Gaines

Most of us would agree that some topics, like religion and art, are influenced by how we see them. But some of us like to think that other topics, like history and science, contain only cold, hard facts, but that is not always true. For example, a lot of so-called history is written by people who want to influence future thinking, not necessarily pass along the facts. Think about the history you were taught about the American Indians. Think about how black culture in America has been recorded. In short, history often reflects the way the writers of the history books saw things or want readers to see things, not necessarily the way things actually were.

And what about science? It is empirical. It is based on observation and experiment, not on individual differences. Well, maybe not, because observation is done by individuals, and individuals do not see things the same way. Many observed the heavens before Copernicus without seeing what he saw, and many refused to see things his way for a long time. Many observed nature before Darwin without seeing what he saw, and many still do not see things the way he did. I think the individual must be considered even in science, especially in abstract areas such as cosmology, quantum mechanics, and neurology, where individualism can creep in. Math may come closest to representing reality without being influenced by the individual, but even some areas of math are abstract and subject to being seen as we are.

An Agnostic's Path to God

I think religion is a classic example of this "how we see things" statement. Religion is not about things the way they are; it is about things the way we are. There are some common beliefs in the various religions and their subsets, but to a large extent, religion is personal. You can read and study and listen all your life, but you will still see whatever god you believe in the way you are, not the way he may be. This is not meant as an argument against religion. It is simply meant as a philosophical way of understanding religious beliefs.

Three

Religion 2

The theme of this chapter is the same as the previous one. Since there was so much to say about religion, I thought two chapters would be appropriate.

My Way Okay

As stated in the introduction, public opinion surveys indicate that over 90 percent of Americans say they believe in God, and this percentage has been consistent since the 1950s, when the surveys began. The same surveys show that not as many believe in heaven, hell, miracles, and other concepts related to God, and not nearly as many attend church regularly. But it is remarkable that more than nine out of ten Americans believe that God exists. Admittedly, public opinion does not necessarily reflect reality, but public opinion does reflect what people believe.

Why do my beliefs differ from those of so many people? I gave a few reasons in the introduction, but maybe the truth is I am out of touch with reality or just not smart enough to understand. When you disagree with the overwhelming majority of people, it is a little intimidating, because there is a good chance you are wrong. Maybe I am just plain wrong to question the logic of believing in God.

I have thought about this most of my life. I have read extensively and continue to read on a variety of theistic, scientific, and other topics related to the concept of God. And I pride myself on having an open mind and being willing to accept the truth, regardless of the source and regardless of the pain the truth might cause. I certainly am not driven by some underlying desire to discredit religion or those who believe in God. I am driven by an overwhelming desire to know the truth.

Still, I do not want to be viewed as a bad or evil person. I do not want to be labeled as someone who is without moral values or character. I know I am far from perfect, but I am not bad, evil, cruel, or mean. So I try to console myself. I reason that my thirst for truth is acceptable, because if there is a god, he instilled in me the need to question the norm, and if there is not a god, I have reason to doubt.

Death in Design
Belief in God holds the promise of life after death. According to the Christian, Muslim, and Jewish holy books, if you live

your life as God wants, after you die you will be resurrected and live in heaven forever. However, if you do not live your life as God wants, you could spend time in hell. The point is that the big reward or punishment comes after you die, and since information following death is nonexistent, there is no way of knowing for certain if the belief is correct. And logic requires that we be leery of believing something that cannot be checked or verified in some way. (Some have claimed they died, went to heaven, and returned, but their stories are suspect, as discussed elsewhere. I have not read any accounts of anyone dying, going to hell, and returning.)

We cannot automatically say a belief is wrong just because it cannot be readily verified. Verification could eliminate doubt, but it is not necessarily a requirement for a belief to be valid. However, we must recognize that we are subject to deception if we accept beliefs that cannot be proven. We can point to words in a book or faith in our hearts, but such proof is not absolute. Such proof is subjective. Unless a belief can be proven by objective means, doubt remains.

In large part this line of thinking gets back to the issue of faith, but in some ways, it goes beyond that. It goes to the design or substance of the belief. Many beliefs have come and gone because they could not stand the test of time. Constant examination revealed flaws that proved the belief wrong. But a belief that is impossible to prove wrong could last indefinitely. Again, that does not necessarily make it wrong, but it makes it suspect.

What the Commandments Command

The Ten Commandments are thought to be a summary of God's law and are therefore paramount in Jewish, Christian, and even Islamic principles. They are at the core of religious doctrine, dogma, and ethics. But the commandments actually embrace two very different subjects. The commandments contain some moral principles that most of us agree with, but they also promote a theistic theme that some of us do not accept. This mixing of moral doctrine with religious dogma is unfortunate because it creates divisiveness and controversy.

The first four commandments promote theism, or belief in God, putting him first, and honoring him:

1. I am God; put no others before me.
2. Make no graven images.
3. Do not misuse my name.
4. Keep the Sabbath holy.

The other commandments are not necessarily religious. They are logical, universal values:

5. Honor your parents.
6. Do not kill.
7. Do not commit adultery.
8. Do not steal.
9. Do not lie.
10. Do not covet.

Most people, regardless of their religion or lack thereof, recognize and accept the values embraced by the nontheistic commandments. But the theistic commandments portray God in a controlling, needy way.

God's neediness is reflected in his attitude. He seems short-tempered and intolerant of anyone who does not understand or accept his message. And unfortunately, much of his teachings are not direct but are vague or are based on parables, figures of speech, or wording that lack clarity and could be taken different ways. Indeed, much of what he said and did is subject to interpretation and is taken different ways by different people. Yet we are expected to understand his point immediately or suffer his wrath. The Bible talks of him killing the firstborn, unleashing a plague on thousands, and even punishing future generations for what someone did. The Quran talks of painful chastisement for various offenses. God seems to rule by power and fear instead of love and logic. I think a kind and benevolent god would be more tolerant, patient, and clear, and logic tells me to be leery of heavy-handed, self-focused behavior.

Unfortunately, many religious people exhibit this same intolerant attitude toward those of us who question their beliefs. I believe God and his followers would be better served if they were more tolerant of ignorance, differing opinions, and diversity. Those of us who question are not necessarily bad people. We simply cannot accept God as portrayed in the holy books.

Choices, Choices

The fact that there are so many different religions and so many branches or subsets of each is evidence that no one belief is necessarily right, because if there were a god and his direction was clear and logical, most people would eventually believe the same way. After all, most of us accept some things as universal truths or end points that our knowledge, experience, and logic have taken us to. But there are no universal religious end points or truths.

There are many different types of nonbelievers too, from secularists and agnostics to avowed atheists. These diverse beliefs among the religious and nonreligious alike point to not only a lack of universal truth but also to the differences in people. I think they are proof that "we see things as we are." Religious beliefs or lack thereof are very personal and exemplify a reflection of self, or seeing things as we are.

No Church for Agnostics

Agnostics do not have to meet regularly to confirm or reaffirm or broadcast their beliefs. I know some people need to participate in group activity, and there is nothing wrong with that. But when the group activity is seen as mandatory regarding something as basic as personal beliefs, and when the activity is driven by repetitive rite, ritual, and dogma and devoid of objective criticism, I wonder about its value. For agnostics, there is no rule to pray, vocalize, contribute, pretend, socialize, proselytize, have a structured bureaucracy, tithe, and so forth. The beliefs stand on their own.

Faith and Love

I have heard some defend religious faith by comparing it to human love. They say that as with religious faith, you cannot prove human love in empirical terms, yet we know it exists. Admittedly, love for another human being may be a little like religious faith in that it is not necessarily logical or provable. However, unlike religious faith, human love grows from personal experiences with a tangible human being. It does not require the acceptance of contradictory documents or supernatural events or questionable dogma. (And there is a big difference between loving and worshiping too.)

Religious Bullying

I knew a Christian woman who needed a kidney transplant. A relative offered to provide one, but she declined, even though his was a perfect match. She said she declined because the relative was not a Christian. Was she afraid that by accepting she might contribute to the donor going to hell if he died during the operation? Was she concerned about putting a non-Christian part in her body? Maybe there were other reasons, but in any case, I have often wondered about her decision. I know she was a genuinely good person and would never knowingly bully, coerce, or otherwise be unkind to someone. But it seemed to me she was controlling another's behavior based on her religious beliefs. I do not question her right to be religious and can understand how her beliefs would influence her decisions. But I have often wondered how the man who offered his kidney felt. Did he feel controlled, put down, unappreciated? I think I would, if I offered to give part of my body to save someone's life and was turned down. I believe this is an example of how religion can drive us apart. I do not believe anyone was at fault here, but I believe religion turned a noble gesture into a conundrum.

A broader example is the issue of gay marriage. The Bible is clear on sodomy, and many oppose gay marriage for religious reasons. Instead of objectively considering the matter based on compassion, fairness, or equity, religious teachings thousands of years old are used. (Such teachings have also been used to defend unequal treatment of women, slavery, and other behavior that is now considered undesirable.)

This is a good place to mention that the Bible is also clear on divorce, gluttony, greed, coveting, and other behaviors that are widely practiced. It seems the formula is to use the Bible to define the sins we hate, but do not mention what the Bible says about the ones we practice. This allows us to practice religious bullying without being perfect.

Two Wrongs

I read a book recently written by a minister who admitted that a lot of evil had been done in the name of religion. He referenced the Crusades, the Inquisition, the present-day suicide bombers who call themselves martyrs, and others. But then he went on to say that a lot of evil has also been done in secular societies, and he mentioned the Communists and the Nazis as examples. He tried to make the point that evil was not necessarily caused by religion. And I agree. All evil is not caused by religion. Only some of it.

God Is What

Some say that God is love. It is hard to see the logic of that statement. The Old Testament of the Bible describes a God who was demanding, vengeful, homophobic, jealous, mean-spirited, and controlling. It related events where he killed the innocent and committed, promoted, or allowed infanticide, genocide, and homicide. He unleashed plagues on the general population because of decisions made by their leaders, and he was often oblivious to all but his chosen people and even turned on them at times. He promoted the slaughter of animals, punished people for things done by their ancestors, was fond of the smell of burning flesh, and was vague and reclusive. So how could we say God is love?

The New Testament softened God's image some, but even Jesus seemed selective, vague, secretive, and unwilling to use his powers in grand ways. Although walking on water or turning water to wine would demonstrate supernatural powers, such acts seem showy more than anything. He did heal some people and even raise the dead, but only on select occasions. And talking in parables or performing miracles on select occasions does not seem especially helpful. He even urged followers to put him ahead of their families, a practice that seems self-focused and cruel.

Maybe we could truthfully say that God has shown love or that God is capable of love or that Jesus taught love, but to say that God is love is inconsistent with the Bible. In fact I think you would be hard-pressed to find a character, real or fictional, in all of history, who perpetuated more atrocities or laid the groundwork for more pain and suffering than God. To say that God is love is to ignore what the Bible says about God.

No Pets Allowed

Could we be united in heaven with the pets we had on earth? Certainly, there could be animals in heaven if God wanted there to be, but could those animals be the same ones we had on earth? Supposedly human beings are the only animals with a soul, which is necessary for life after death, according to the Abrahamic religions. So if Spot, Fluffy, and Wiggles do not have souls, how do they get to heaven? Logic tells me that if a soul is required to get to heaven and if pets do not have souls, we will not see our pets in heaven. (Maybe we will see cloned versions of them, but that is another issue.) Could heaven be perfect without our pets?

The Myth Goes On

I believe most religious people were raised in religious households, or at least they were exposed to religious beliefs at an early age. I also believe that most religious people practice the same or similar religion that they were exposed to during their childhood. If these are fair statements, then it is also fair to say that religion is based on beliefs that are taught, not necessarily on beliefs that are the result of a search for truth.

Generally, children raised in Christian households do not grow up to become Muslims. And children raised in Jewish households do not grow up to become Hindus. This is understandable. We believe what we are taught, especially during our formative years. Unless we come to question religious teachings at an early age, we do not feel comfortable with calling ourselves agnostics or atheists or nonreligious. Unless we somehow learn to search for truth by applying logic and reason and to always be skeptical of any supernatural claims, we accept the religion of our parents. In fact, many are taught that to question or be skeptical of religious doctrine is wrong, so even if they are not devout, they are loath to admit it.

What Preachers Preach

Many of us have witnessed or experienced the misuse of power by an officer of the law, a government bureaucrat, or others in positions of authority. The misuse of power is an attempt to control the behavior of others. In fact, many who seek to control others seek professions that give them some measure of authority. I am not saying that all police officers or government regulators are control freaks. I am just saying that such positions attract those who seek to control. Good people in positions of power apply their power objectively, in accordance with the rules that apply, and without personal agendas, but those in positions of power who seek to control misuse their authority.

I believe some people use religious tenets as a means of control. They use religion to control the behavior of others. There is nothing wrong with sharing sincere religious beliefs, but many who preach or otherwise attempt to instill religious beliefs in others do so out of a desire to control, not necessarily to spread God's word. Piety can be strong and pure and good, but sanctimony is dark and insidious. I believe sanctimonious behavior in an effort to control others is a form of bullying. And I believe those who practice it are as detestable as the police officers or bureaucrats who misuse their authority.

I also think some preachers use religion as a means to get attention, promote personal agendas, and gain wealth. Some are like actors or politicians who crave attention and turn their performances into spectacles. Some have a personal agenda and weave it into their sermons in the guise of religious doctrine. Perhaps the most notorious are those who solicit money in the name of religion but channel it to personal use.

If you want to learn about religion, do not just rely on what others say. Read the Bible or Quran or other credible religious documents. Read them over and over and study them and think about them. Read other related material from a variety of sources and apply critical, analytical reasoning and logic to sort out the truth. Above all, be leery of what preachers preach. (Beware of false prophets!)

Sin and Guilt

Not having been a practicing Jew, Muslim, or Christian, I cannot say from firsthand experience what goes on in their places of worship. My only experience with going to church came as a child when my grandparents would occasionally take me to a small Baptist church in my hometown of Dexter, Missouri. What I remember most from the few times I attended was the emphasis on sin and guilt. The preaching, teaching, and overall philosophy seemed to spin around sin, from the so-called original sin of Adam and Eve, to the abundance of ongoing sins in everyday life. I remember hearing how sinful we all are and what guilt we should feel and how terribly we sinners will be treated in the hereinafter. I was only five or six years old, and the fire and brimstone rhetoric made a lasting impression. I was taught to feel guilt without understanding what I had done wrong, and I was made to fear an eternity of burning in hell that could result not necessarily from being a bad person but from simply not practicing certain rituals. In short, my experience left me with a negative uncertainty that haunted me for years.

Logic tells me and experience showed me that religious teachings that focus heavily on sin, guilt, and fear will not produce happy people. (I do not think anyone in that church felt really happy there!) I believe people would be better served if they were enlightened rather than chastised, taught to feel joy rather than shame, and encouraged to think highly of themselves and others rather than made to focus so much on sin, guilt, and fear. Logic tells me that if religion serves a good purpose, it is to make people feel more secure and happy; however, the sin and guilt parts do just the opposite.

God's Will

Anytime someone refers to the will of God, be careful. Feel sympathy for people if they are trying to find comfort by attributing events to God's will. That is based on faith, and it probably does little harm or poses little threat to invoke his will in ways that are not critical of others. But feel threatened if people invoke God's will in an attempt to criticize others or change their behavior.

If there is a god, no mortal could know his will. To seriously assert otherwise would be the height of arrogance. Clergy, theologians, or other religious people may assert that they know the will of God based on what they think God has done or said in the past, but their assertions are flawed. First, most religious documents are imperfect, and second, even if they were perfect and absolute, how they are interpreted is subjective. No mortal can know the will of any god, except perhaps someone who has had personal interactions with him, as some prophets and others have claimed.

In short, invoking the will of God and pointing to the Bible or the Quran or other writings as proof is not convincing, and those who do so are probably trying to be manipulative. Strong positions are made evident by observation, experiment, empirical data, logical thought, and so forth, not by pretending to know God's will. Be suspicious of anyone claiming to know God's will.

Priorities

Some religions divert much wealth to materialistic or frivolous things, as evidenced by their buildings, ceremonies, attire, and bureaucratic structure. While this is not necessarily a bad thing and certainly does not diminish the credibility of religious beliefs, it does speak to the priorities that are embraced by the followers.

The Troublesome Tenth

The Bible's tenth commandment warns against coveting, or wanting what is not ours. It is one of those "thou shalt not" commandments, like the ones on making graven images, killing, stealing, and lying, except that it prohibits a mental act, not a physical one. The commandments on remembering the Sabbath and honoring of parents primarily involve mental acts, but arguably more controllable ones. I do not think any of us can fully control our thoughts, and I do not think some random, innocent coveting is necessarily bad. In fact, wanting what we do not have can be motivation for improvement. In short, I think all of the other nine commandments can be mostly obeyed with conscious effort, but I do not think the tenth can. Regardless of how much faith, devotion, or commitment we have, I do not think we can keep a random covet from entering our minds. Hence, maybe we are all doomed to hell simply by being alive.

Or maybe when God came up with the Ten Commandments, he intended the tenth one to be something like this: Thou shalt not covet in ways that lead to evil deeds. Many of us have wanted something we did not have but have never followed up on the want because we knew it would be immoral, illegal, or otherwise wrong. Surely there is nothing wrong with having uncontrollable, random wants that do not lead to actions. And many of us have wanted something better for ourselves or our family and have worked in admirable ways to get it. Surely there is nothing wrong with that.

Logically, it is not the thought that is wrong but what the thought can lead to.

Trouble with Angels

Angels are mentioned in the holy books and other places. Descriptions vary, but they seem to be supernatural beings with greater than human power who often serve as messengers of God or as guardians or who in some way influence human affairs or behavior. They are often depicted as having wings and a halo. Angels have the general reputation of being good; hence, we sometimes refer to someone, especially a female, as an angel, to compliment her. But angels can be bad too, as with Satan or the angel of death or the Muslims' jinn. Perhaps angels were invented to fill the wide gap between us and God. At times when God wants something done but does not want to do it personally, he can use angels. They have power beyond ours but certainly not on his level.

The concept of angels raises many questions: Where do they come from? Where do they reside? Are there a specific number of them? Do they procreate? Are they temporary or permanent? Do they have mass? Do they need food?

Logic tells me that the concept of angels is yet another ill-defined fantasy associated with religious belief that can be neither proven nor disproven. (However, I am not opposed to calling a female an angel to compliment her.)

Religion the Easy Way

Some people who are not devout or even religious get defensive if they perceive a religious slight. Extreme examples are the terrorists who take lives in the name of religion. But less extreme and more common examples include those who complain if they cannot exhibit their religious messages on public property; those who say their speech is limited if they cannot verbalize prayer in government settings; those who object when some branch of government tries to keep religion out of public policy; and those who feel public policy goes against their religious beliefs in some way. Why would otherwise nonreligious people publicly defend religion? It does not seem logical. Maybe they do so because it allows them to be religious without having to change.

What better way to show the world you are a person of substance than to get indignant over a perceived slight of your religion? What better way to make amends for your sins or your guilt than to publicly support your religion? And you can do this without having to change anything about yourself, make any sacrifices, or do anything you do not want to do. You do not have to change your ways, ask forgiveness, make commitments, admit fault, pray, or do any of those things that require you to take ownership of your behavior. You can just put yourself on the side of what is undoubtedly true and holy by taking a stand against religious injustice. It is quick and easy and painless.

More Than We Can Handle

Would we be given more than we can handle? Of course we would. People get more than they can handle all the time. That is why some people are stressed or depressed, why some commit suicide, and why some commit atrocities or go insane. Anyone who says God would never give us more than we can handle is just repeating an inaccurate cliché.

Chaos and Change

There is a secular side of the Bible. The best evidence is found in one of the most-quoted verses from the Bible, which comes from perhaps the most out-of-place book of the Bible. To quote Ecclesiastes 9:11, which pretty much expresses my philosophy on the way things work:

> "Again, I saw, under the sun, that the race is not to the swift, or the battle to the strong, or bread to the wise, or riches to the discerning, or favor to the skillful; rather, time and chance happen to them all."

In other words, chaos rules.

This verse also illustrates that the Bible is subject to change. I memorized the verse, since I liked it so much, and when I would come across it in different Bibles, I would notice that it was often stated differently from my memorized version. In fact, I have seen it stated numerous ways.

Admittedly, the different wordings convey pretty much the same general meaning, but the fact that so many different versions exist shows me that the Bible is subject to change. And then I got to thinking: If there are many versions of this one little verse that I like so much, what about the whole Bible? How many Bible verses are in their original form? How much of the original meaning has been changed, either by error or on purpose?

The Chosen Few

The Bible and the Quran indicate that God chose Abraham to be the patriarch of God's people. Jews think they are special because they are descendants of Abraham's son Isaac. Muslims think they are special because their holy prophet Muhammad was a descendent of Abraham's oldest son, Ishmael. And Christians think they are special because their messiah, Jesus, was a descendent of King David, who was a descendent of Abraham and Isaac. If the Bible and the Quran are accurate, then Jews, Muslims, and Christians all have a legitimate reason to think they are special in God's eyes. But logic tells me that if there is a god, he values all people equally.

Democracy and a Supreme Being

As indicated elsewhere, over 90 percent of the people in America who respond to the polls say they believe in a supreme being. This pretty much assures that no atheist, agnostic, or nonbeliever could get elected to public office unless the candidate kept his or her beliefs hidden. It also ensures that some politicians will try to align themselves with a supreme being to get votes. It is shameful and manipulative, but it works. Not all politicians with a religious agenda are manipulative, but some do use religious rhetoric to attract votes, especially in areas with a lot of evangelical voters, and especially on issues with a religious undertone such as abortion, gay rights, and terrorism.

Almost all elected officials in the United States are outwardly religious. Atheists, agnostics, and nonbelievers have negligible representation in government. The process is insidious because it sways our democracy toward a theocracy. We talk about the separation of church and state, but separation is almost impossible as long as we have a religious litmus test for politicians.

Some even argue that our constitution was heavily influenced by Christian beliefs. That is a valid argument since some of the framers were Christians and would naturally pull from their religious beliefs to write a guiding document. But I do not think that just because our constitution was influenced by Christianity, we should feel that other religions or beliefs are inappropriate or in any way secondary. The Constitution speaks for itself. We do not need to factor in the faith of the framers.

An Agnostic's Path to God

The United States is the most religious of any developed nation. Many other developed nations, especially in Europe, have become more secular over the years, but we have not. I am not saying that for our country to be religious is wrong. Not at all. Freedom of religion is one of our basic tenets. But I believe in freedom from religion too, and that is hard to come by in this country at times. Our money, pledges, oaths, issues, and leaders all keep religion in front of us.

Bankruptcy

Some religions are morally bankrupt because of past and ongoing transgressions. The Catholic Church is an example, with its history of torturing and killing nonbelievers and its recent and ongoing practice of protecting priests who are pedophiles. That is not to say that those who practice such religions are bad, only that their churches exhibit some bad behavior. The laity does not necessarily condone the bad behavior; I believe it just tolerates the behavior in hopes of a greater good.

Similarly, religious terrorism is abhorrent, but that does not necessarily mean the religion is bad. Terrorism is a product of radical behavior by people who hate, not a product of how most of the religion's believers feel. The present-day terrorists can be compared to the crusaders of the middle ages who tortured, burned, and killed people for not being Christian, but we know that the crusaders were not reflective of Christian behavior. Logic tells me that violence done in the name of religion is more about the dark side of humanity than religion.

Familiarity Breeds Reality

Religious people who urge nonbelievers to read the Bible or other religious documents are smart. They know that if you are exposed to something enough, you are more likely to accept it as truth. They know that truth, or reality, has to do with repetition, perception, and familiarity. I am an example. Over a period of many years, I have read and reread the Bible, Quran, and many other religious books. I have thought about them, discussed them, visualized them, written about them, and questioned them so much that some of the events and characters actually seem real. Certainly some of the places mentioned are real, and some of the events and characters could be real. Therefore, it is not a big leap to start believing the whole narrative, including the supernatural parts. Put some fantasy in the lives of some believable people at some real locations, and after a while, the fantasy does not sound so outrageous.

Although I do not think Adam and Eve or Noah or Moses actually existed, I must admit that the Garden of Eden, the flood, and the Exodus stories stick in my mind. And I think of Abraham, Isaac, and Jacob, along with the twelve tribes, whenever I think of present-day Israel. And King David seems almost real, because he was so good and so bad, kind of like a real person. The Bible is full of bigger-than-life characters and events, and the more you read it, the more you identify with those characters and events. Whether we are religious or not, constant exposure to religious stories has made many of us think the stories are true. The Bible and the Quran are great books, and you cannot help but be influenced by them. And the more you read them, the more you are influenced, whether you are religious or not.

It Is No Sacrifice

I used to think people with strong religious beliefs were making sacrifices now in hopes of getting rewards later. I no longer believe that, for several reasons. First, doing the right thing has its own rewards. Whether you follow the Ten Commandments or your own moral code that contains the golden rule, the non-proselytizing commandments, and other good rules to live by, virtue has its blessings. Doing the right thing makes you feel good whether you are religious or not.

Second, looking forward to eternity in paradise is pleasing in itself. It helps remove the fear and uncertainty of death and would make the end much easier. Third, having the peace of mind of an accepted belief system brings happiness now. Fourth, prayer is relaxing, kind of like meditating, and can unwind, settle, and relax the mind. And there are many other benefits to being religious, even if there is no supreme being or afterlife.

I now believe that being religious is not a burden. It is a blessing. Going to church, fasting, praying, following ritual, and many of the other things that go with being religious are not sacrifices if that is what you believe in. I even think that if you could choose whether to be religious or not without having to accept certain parts, then choose to be religious. And if you could even choose the type of religion you wanted, choose Christianity or Islam, since both promise an afterlife. The Christians and Muslims who are devout and morally sound are indeed fortunate.

Four

Christianity

This chapter is not meant to single out Christianity for extra criticism but simply to make a few comments that would not fit elsewhere. Christians embrace the New Testament of the Bible and believe Jesus Christ was the Messiah, and this belief is unique among the Abrahamic religions. There are many different interpretations of the New Testament, leading to many different Christian churches, the largest being the Catholic Church. Most of the comments in this chapter apply to all of Christianity; however, a few apply only to Catholicism.

Even though I am an agnostic, I believe that some of the comments attributed to Jesus in the New Testament provide profound statements on morality. His sermons, parables, and other teachings and his general lifestyle as described in the

New Testament are exemplary. I do not think Jesus was the Messiah, God, or the son of God, but certainly he was a giant in human history and gave us some of the best words to live by ever spoken. I have nothing but deep reverence for him, and the comments on Christianity are not meant to reflect poorly on Jesus in any way.

Books have been written contending that Jesus did not exist as a real person but was conjured up by those who wanted to create a religion. Those who hold such beliefs are called mythicists. As I have said before, I am not a religious or historical scholar, but I do think Jesus the man did exist. However, he may have been reinvented after his death, being transformed from a kingdom of God zealot to the savior of humankind by Paul and others. And, as you might guess, books have been written on that subject too. Much has even been written questioning whether the Gospels represent original work, if any of them were written by the individuals named, or if any represent eyewitness accounts of events. But I try to hold true to my strategy of using logic to base my comments on and leave the reality of Jesus to others who are more qualified to address the issues involved.

Why Die for Me

The Crucifixion of Jesus and some of the events leading up to it are among the most bizarre, gruesome, and bloody parts of the Bible. What is the logic of having Jesus suffer and die to forgive our sins? If the events had to unfold a certain way to coincide with Old Testament prophecies, then we have to look to God as the source of those prophecies. The prophets supposedly just passed along the word of God. So that raises the following questions: Did God actually plan to sacrifice his own son as described? And if he did, why would God use a pagan ritual of human sacrifice to symbolize forgiveness?

It is just not logical to think that the son of God had to undergo humiliation, suffering, and death because we are sinners. The Old Testament describes animal sacrifices to God as a path to forgiveness of sins. That is bad enough. But to think that God wanted to use human sacrifice to symbolize forgiveness is beyond bad. If God wanted to symbolize forgiveness, he could have done so in a more constructive, believable, and positive way. He could have let Jesus stay around and perform miracles, eliminate suffering, or make everyone happy. In short, he could have made heaven on earth. What better way to show forgiveness than to make everyone happy and safe? I know we cannot second-guess God, but it is just not logical to use an excruciating ordeal involving blood drinking, flogging, crucifixion, and a questionable resurrection to make the most important statement in all of Christianity. Positive, provable actions would have been much more logical.

Part of the ordeal leading up to the Crucifixion and resurrection took place at the Last Supper when Jesus asked the apostles to consume his flesh and blood. This seems not only illogical but macabre as well. How could the consumption of flesh and blood, even symbolically, relate to our sins? The ritual, although bizarre, is even part of present-day practice with some Christians.

And what about the Crucifixion itself? It would not be the same for an immortal person as it would be for you or me. If you knew for certain you would come back to life in a few days, what fear would death hold? Certainly a painful death would not be enjoyable, but it would not hold the fear of the unknown that we mortals face. It would just be a painful, gruesome ordeal that you had to endure. Not to trivialize the Crucifixion, but people suffer agonizing deaths all the time from various diseases, tragedies, wars, and so on. And they do so without knowing for certain what lies beyond.

The Crucifixion also gives us one of the most illogical statements in all of religion: "For God so loved the world that he gave his one and only son, that whoever believes in him shall not perish but have eternal life." First, according to the Bible, God did not *give* his only son but only lent him for a while. Jesus ended up in heaven after his ordeal, so it was only a loan. But more importantly, stated another way, the sentence says that God so loved the world that he tortured and killed his only son...This is beyond illogical. It is nonsense. To say that love drove you to torture and kill someone sounds more like what terrorists say. And not only that but he did it so that eternal life would be possible if we would just believe in him. Sometimes I really wonder if parts of the holy books exist just to test us to see if we will accept such illogical, nonsensical characterizations of God. As I have said elsewhere, more than anything else, I cannot accept the Abrahamic god because of the way he is portrayed in the holy books, and the events surrounding the death and resurrection of Jesus exemplify such unacceptable behavior.

In summary, either God planned to sacrifice his son, or the Old Testament is not his word. And if God's plan was to symbolize forgiveness by sacrificing his son, we are left to wonder why he chose such a barbaric ritual. It seems to me that one of Christianity's core beliefs is utter nonsense, and I just cannot believe a good god would act that way.

Looks Can Be Deceiving

It is not logical to portray Jesus as a Caucasian, yet that is what we invariably see. Jesus was a Jew from an Arab country. He would have had olive skin, black hair, and perhaps a broad nose and stocky build, similar to the modern-day Arab. But we see him pictured with light skin; a long, thin nose; a tall, lean build; and other features that are more reflective of a European than a Middle Eastern Jew.

Admittedly, this is a petty issue. It does not diminish the credibility of the core beliefs one bit, but I think it is indicative of how disingenuous some of the religious dogma can be.

And you have to wonder, if something so petty and obvious is obfuscated, what can we believe about the big stuff? When the picture on the wall is deceitful, how credible is the message from the pulpit?

What Purpose Hell
Hell is to scare the devil out of people.

Immaculate Conception(s)
According to the Bible, Mary gave birth to Jesus while still a virgin. Certainly a virgin birth would be a supernatural event and would contribute to the belief that Jesus was the son of God. Was Mary really a virgin when Jesus was born? The Bible is the only source of information we have on that event, but in today's world, it appears that many pregnant women routinely claim to be virgins.

According to a report published in late 2013 in the *BMJ*, Britain's medical journal, nearly 1 percent of pregnant women studied in the United States claimed to be virgins. The report was based on interviews of thousands of women, and the data was analyzed by researchers at the University of North Carolina at Chapel Hill. The reported number of "virgin" pregnancies was forty-five and did not include pregnancies from in vitro fertilizations or other assisted reproductive technology.

Obviously there are issues of sex education, truth telling, memory, and so forth, here, but in this discrete snapshot, many women claimed to be pregnant independent of a man's participation. Multiply this by all pregnancies for all time, and think of how many pregnant women claimed to be virgins. This is not meant to discredit Mary, mother of Jesus. This is only meant to show that many pregnant women have claimed to be virgins over the years.

Papal Power

No treatise of this nature would be complete without a word about papal infallibility. It seems the Vatican Council voted in 1870 that the pope is infallible when he defines doctrines of faith or morals from his throne. Now who would have thought that someone could be made infallible by a vote of mere mortals? The whole concept of God being infallible is based on God being a supreme being. For an earthly group to think it has the ability to create infallibility gives insight into just how illogical and arrogant the thinking can become.

In fairness, I am going to assume that the Vatican Council was essentially saying that when the pope rules on certain matters, the discussion is closed. I am sure the council members were intelligent people and knew the pope was not God. They called it papal infallibility to define a process where a final decision would stand without challenge. I guess I can understand the need of that, but they should have called it something else to avoid creating an oxymoron of monumental proportions.

Mono What

Christians speak of the Trinity, meaning God (the father), Jesus (the son), and the Holy Spirit or Holy Ghost, but say theirs is a monotheistic religion. They say there is only one God in three distinct persons, but the persons are consubstantial, meaning they are of one being or one essence. Although this seems contrived, and *consubstantial* sounds like a made-up word, in some ways it can make sense. If there is a god, he can take whatever form he wants and can change forms if he wants. But in other ways, the logic gets blurred because the Gospels indicate that there are multiple distinct entities.

Jesus talked of the father several times and even said no one gets to the father except through him. If there is only one being or essence, who was Jesus talking about when he spoke of the father? And who was Jesus talking to when he addressed God before the Crucifixion and while on the cross? Who was God talking about when Jesus was baptized and God said he was pleased with Jesus? And what about when Jesus said the father would send the Holy Ghost in his name? And what about the reference to Jesus sitting on the right hand of God when he ascended to heaven? Also why refer to the father, the son, and the Holy Spirit when addressing God if all are one and the same? It appears that in some instances, more than one Godlike entity exits at the same time.

The Christian doctrine of the Trinity is difficult to understand and accept, and that is why some refer to Christianity as being a polytheistic religion. As indicated above, the New Testament has wording implying that multiple Godlike entities exist at the same time. And polytheism comes to mind even more when the apostles are given supernatural powers and when Mary, mother of Jesus, is revered to the highest by the largest Christian church.

This is a good place to question why many Christians feel monotheism is superior to polytheism. If I were a Christian and felt the need to defend my religion, I would say "so what." Polytheism has distinct advantages over monotheism, such as having specialty gods or a hierarchy of gods, or not making one god so aloof and unreachable, or even having the father, son, and Holy Spirit trinity. Maybe Christians should embrace the polytheistic label as an advantage instead of something undesirable.

The Question of Resurrection

The resurrection of Jesus is the cornerstone of Christianity. The miracles, the healing, and other supernatural events described in the New Testament all point to a messiah, but without the resurrection, Christianity falls apart. However, there are problems with the resurrection stories, and perhaps the biggest one is that some apostolic accounts point to a physical resurrection of Jesus, and some point to a spiritual one. A physical resurrection is much more compelling for proving that Jesus was a messiah because a spiritual resurrection or ascension is thought to occur when some mortals die. This inconsistency creates doubt as to whether Jesus's resurrection was real or figurative.

But even if we assume that the more compelling physical resurrection with witnesses took place, there are problems. Certainly if Jesus Christ did die and come back to life, he was other than human. But there are several logical reasons for doubting this really happened. Some have speculated that Jesus did not die on the cross but simply passed out or went into a coma, and then he regained consciousness in the tomb. Others say the sightings of Christ after the Crucifixion were actually cases of mistaken identity, sightings of a look-alike, or maybe even a planned ruse.

Others say that since the earliest New Testament accounts of the resurrection were not written for a generation or more after it allegedly occurred, their accuracy is questionable, and they probably are embellished accounts of events rather than actual happenings. Others say the accounts pull from a common source and do not independently verify actual events. Others say that since the accounts were written only by close followers of Jesus, they do not represent objective descriptions of the events surrounding him but were written to promote and enhance his image. Others say the accounts were revised many times over the years to promote acceptance of Christianity and therefore are not a reliable source of information. In short, from the time the accounts of a resurrection were written, there have been many differences of opinion as to what they actually say and mean.

Even though the New Testament writings make a reasonable case for a resurrection having occurred, they do not eliminate all doubt, and this leads to the question of why so many people accept Christianity when there is doubt about the cornerstone of Christian beliefs. As already stated, I believe many accept religious tenets because of the promise of life after death, and of course Christianity provides such a promise. That has great appeal. If you believe, you can give yourself to Christ and diminish the fears and uncertainty of death. You can even look forward to being united with loved ones in heaven after death. It is very enticing. It is not driven by logic. It is driven by the desire for an afterlife.

Would Christians worship Jesus if there were no promise of eternal life? (Muslims believe in an afterlife without believing in the resurrection of Jesus.)

Resurrection Part II

Even if the events described in the New Testament are true, that is still not absolute proof that there is a god and an afterlife in heaven. In other words, even if we accept the miracles and the resurrection, that does not prove there is a god. How can you explain the miracles and the resurrection without a god? I do not know. But not knowing is not proof. If there is a god and Jesus was his son, the New Testament accounts could be true. But could the accounts be true without a god? Maybe. I do not know how, but it is just not logical to assert that some miraculous events regarding Jesus Christ, many of which are questionable and all of which happened almost two thousand years ago, are absolute proof that there is a god.

Many will think this reason is petty, but I argue that it is a logical doubt. Supernatural events, no matter how miraculous, are not proof of a god, even if some of the events were foretold in the Old Testament. (In fact, efforts described in the New Testament to make sure certain events follow prophecies bring credibility into question.) But even if the New Testament described actual events and even if all doubt is eliminated regarding the events, that is still not absolute proof of a god. It is an indication, it is circumstantial evidence, and it is compelling, alluring, and fascinating, but it is not absolute proof. God still has to be taken on faith. Proof of a fact requires objective, repeatable evidence that cannot be refuted. If a million assertions, testimonials, observations, assumptions, and predictions cause us to believe a certain way but one path leads another way, uncertainty exists. Compare this with laws of nature, such as the one that says opposite electrical charges attract each other. Logic forces us to admit that even if the law holds true in a million cases but fails in one, it is no longer a law.

Jesus and Prophecies

Many Christians believe that prophets in the Old Testament foretold of Jesus. Indeed, there are several passages in the Old Testament that speak of a coming messiah, and some provide details regarding his lineage, birth, death, and other events related to him. Are the prophecies evidence of a supreme being?

Certainly, if events were predicted hundreds of years before they occurred, that would be evidence of divine intervention. However, consider the following: There are prophecies in the Old Testament that have not come to pass. And although there are ones related to a coming messiah, many are vague. Their meaning is not clear or could be taken different ways. It is possible that the prophecies have been revised over the eons, calling into question the exact meaning of the original ones. And it is possible that the accounts of the events that were prophesied were contorted to match the prophecies; that is, events could have been described in ways that emphasized what was predicted and minimized or ignored conflicting details. Also, Jesus and others mentioned in the New Testament were very familiar with Old Testament prophecies and could have helped shape events to match them.

In short, without knowing exactly what the original prophecies called for, exactly what happened when a prophesied event took place, and exactly what the intent was of those who had a part in the event or wrote about the event, we cannot say with certainty how accurate the prophecies are. (Perhaps the most famous biblical prophecy that turned out to be wrong was Jesus's statement to some followers that Judgment Day would come during their lifetime.)

Poor Ol' Judas and Others

It does not seem logical that Judas Iscariot should be forever branded as a betrayer and despicable character for his role in Jesus's fate. According to the Bible, Judas identified Jesus to the Romans, which led to Jesus's Crucifixion. But the Bible also makes it clear that Jesus knew Judas was going to betray him but allowed it as part of his overall plan for the salvation of humanity. Therefore, was Judas doing a bad deed, or was he just a pawn? The Crucifixion and resurrection were part of Jesus's plan and are critical to Christian beliefs; therefore, I do not think it is logical to criticize Judas for the part he played. What if Judas had exercised free will and had gone against Jesus's plan? Would Christians be better off? The Bible gives conflicting accounts of Judas's death, but both accounts are very unpleasant. Maybe Christians should be grateful for the scapegoat role Judas played in the whole macabre affair.

Others who played a major part in the Crucifixion have been more or less villainized too. Pontius Pilate, Herod, the chief priests, and others were part of the saga (the Passion), but again, what they did facilitated the plan that Jesus (God) saw ahead of time. So either these characters had no free will and were just part of a divine plan, in which case they were not responsible for their actions, or they were exercising free will, in which case the Passion was not a divine plan but was the outcome of random events. I do not think Judas and the others should be criticized if we accept the Passion as part of God's plan.

Secret Miracles

Several times when Jesus performed miracles, he asked that they be kept secret. That does not seem logical. What better way to convince others that he was the son of God than by performing miracles? It is hard to understand why he would want to keep them secret. It is as if he is saying, "I am the son of God, and the future of humanity will depend on me, but do not tell anyone."

Mass Appeal

Religions in general and Christianity in particular seem to favor the poor. Jesus said it would be easier for a camel to pass through the eye of a needle than for a rich man to get into heaven, and he said woe to the rich for you have received your consolation. Although it is natural to have empathy for the less fortunate, I do not believe it is logical to think they would be favored by a supreme being. Salvation is generally based on faith, acceptance of religious ritual, deeds, or matters of character, not on income or wealth. To imply that wealth undermines what is needed for salvation is not logical. I think the implication is that most wealthy people exhibit bad behavior in obtaining their wealth, but that is not a logical implication. I dare say the poor exhibit as much bad behavior as the wealthy. One does not justify the other, and both are equally bad.

I believe the inventors of religion simply wanted to cater to those less fortunate, knowing there would be greater appeal to the masses by doing so because more of us are poor than rich. The poor may like to hear that it would be hard for a rich man to get to heaven because that is salve for being poor. But it is not logical to think that the rich are evil and the poor are good. If the logic of faith, ritual, deeds, or character is kept pure, and if we view God as loving all of humankind without discriminating, wealth would not enter in.

I think most of us agree that those of us who are able should help those who are less fortunate. And I think we agree that any form of oppressive treatment of people is bad. But I do not think it is logical to judge people or make implications as to their morality based on their material worth. Wealth per se is not a sin. Behaving inappropriately to accumulate wealth is wrong, but wealth itself is not.

Is Doubting Wrong

The apostles did not believe Jesus had risen when Mary Magdalene and others told them so. And when they saw the risen Jesus and he stood among them, they were afraid. And apostle Thomas, who was not with the others when they first saw the risen Jesus, would not believe Jesus had risen even when the other apostles told him so. Thomas had to see and touch Jesus himself before believing, hence the name Doubting Thomas. The apostles had known Jesus and had heard him preach and teach and had witnessed him perform miracles, yet they did not believe he had risen. Therefore, is it any wonder that some of us who came along thousands of years later cannot believe either?

The reaction of Doubting Thomas and the other apostles is Biblical proof that faith is not easy when it comes to believing in the supernatural, yet many say we are judged based on faith. What if the apostles had not seen the risen Jesus? What if Thomas had not been able to touch the risen Jesus? Would their lack of faith have condemned them to hell? Logic tells me that some of us cannot accept supernatural events without tangible proof, and it appears the Bible agrees. (In fact, it appears even Jesus thought he had been forsaken by God when he was on the cross. If the son of God loses faith, what chance do we mortals have?)

We All Need One

Saul, aka Paul, had an epiphany on the road to Damascus that changed him. Before the event, Saul persecuted Christians, but after it, he changed his name to Paul and became a Christian. Maybe we all need some kind of life-changing event to erase our doubts and convince us to believe in God. I believe an event such as Paul experienced would be very revealing, and if it happened to Paul, then logically it could happen to any of us. Why would one nonbeliever receive treatment that made him change his beliefs and the rest of us be expected to change without such treatment? Paul appeared to be on the road to hell before his epiphany. Maybe those of us who lack faith would have a change of heart if we experienced a real-life revelation as Paul did.

My Dilemma

There is a warm feeling that comes from believing in God. The feeling cools a little after reading the Bible. It cools a little more after learning some of what has been done in the name of God. It cools a little more with the confusion of God the father, God the son, and God the Holy Spirit. The feeling gets cold when told that God the son, or Jesus, was tortured and crucified to pay for the sins of others. It gets even colder when told that my salvation will depend on my faith in or acceptance of supernatural events, not on what I say or do. I want the warmth; I want to believe—but I do not want the fantasy, cruelty, bloodshed (human and animal), control, discrimination, and illogical thought. Yes, I have a dilemma.

Five

SCIENCE

The following reasons I have trouble believing in God are based on applying generally accepted scientific knowledge, and since such knowledge is often related to correct reasoning or cause and effect, many of the reasons could fit into the logic category too. Some of the reasons have a historical as well as a scientific basis. If reasons are based on scientific principles or knowledge that may not be commonly known, brief explanations are provided. I have tried to avoid being too technical because I do not want to hinder understanding, but since many technical issues do relate directly to religion, it is important to include them.

Test of Time
To some extent belief in God originated, evolved, and exists today because people needed ways to explain some things

that they could not otherwise explain. For example, the holy books contain assertions about the beginning of the universe and the origin of life, and until relatively recently, no other credible source of information on those subjects existed. However, within the last few hundred years, with advances in physics, chemistry, astronomy, cosmology, biology, and other scientific disciplines, credible theories have evolved to explain many phenomena, and there is less need for religious explanations. Certainly, we humans do not have all the answers yet. But as our knowledge grows and understanding broadens, religious explanations will become less and less relevant.

Many questions regarding the beginning of the universe, the origin of life, and other issues remain. And even though there are credible and generally accepted theories that answer some of these questions, they are theories, not proven fact. Their validity, as with most theories, will be determined by the test of time. Expanding knowledge has a way of proving, rejecting, or modifying past attempts to explain reality. Time has a way of separating fact from fiction.

Where Do We Come From

Various theories exist to explain the origin of the universe. How it all began is one of the biggest questions of all time. The three most common theories are creationism, steady state, and the big bang.

Creationists hold that God created the universe, generally as described in the Bible; however, they believe in different timelines. Fundamentalists believe the universe was created a few thousand years ago as described in the Bible, while other creationists have a less literal interpretation of the timeline. All creationists believe that God is the creator of the universe.

The steady state theory holds that the universe has existed for an infinitely long time and therefore had no origin or beginning. It was always here, and no explanation as to how it got here is needed. The steady state theory can be explained with or without a god.

The big bang theory holds that the universe sprang from nothing as a spontaneous quantum flux approximately fifteen billion years ago and expanded and evolved to its present state. Many cosmologists accept some form of the big bang theory because of empirical evidence that has been discovered. The most notable evidence consists of the detection of a cosmic background radiation, thought to be radiation left form the big bang, and the observation that the universe continues to expand. The big bang theory can be explained with or without a god.

Although God is not excluded from any of the theories, the point here is that there are two widely held and credible theories that explain the origin of the universe without the need for divine intervention.

An Agnostic's Path to God

Mortal Clouds

> We are clouds in a gusty sky
> And time is an endless wind
> That erases all traces of our existence
> In spite of our efforts to ease the end
>
> Metal and masonry may make a show
> But neither will long endure
> The metal will rust, the masonry crack
> And their meaning will become obscure
>
> Fame or fortune or great contribution
> May slow the rot, but none will last
> Galaxies churn, worlds collide
> Erasing the relevance of the past
>
> Religion, progeny, invention, and more
> Are marshaled against the end
> But we mortal clouds cannot survive
> The swirling, smiling, beguiling wind

Evolution 101

Polls indicate that about a third of Americans do not believe in evolution. They believe we have always been the way we are now. They do not believe the theories proposed by Darwin that talk of natural selection or survival of the fittest or constantly changing life-forms. They believe we began as we are now. There are many reasons why their beliefs are wrong:

- We know that similar species of animals sometimes interbreed, producing hybrids. (Nearly 10 percent of all bird species are known to occasionally interbreed.) Such hybrids are essentially a new species.
- We know that some microorganisms develop a resistance to antibiotics; that is, they adapt to toxins through natural selection, essentially forming new, resistant organisms.
- We see fossils of life-forms that no longer exist and fossils that show how life-forms have changed with the passage of time.
- We know genes affect future generations and that some genes are favored over others.
- We know that genes sometimes mutate through natural processes, causing changes in future generations.
- We know that genes can respond to stimuli during an organism's lifetime, and this "gene expression" can change the organism's behavior in many ways, either short-term or long-term.
- We know that genetically modified organisms (GMOs), plants and animals whose DNA has been manipulated in a laboratory, are becoming more common.
- We see evidence everywhere that life-forms have been shaped by their environment.

- We know that plants and animals often compete for survival and that those best-suited for a given environment can thrive where others fail.
- We know that many plant and animal species have been changed over the years by selective breeding, crossbreeding, grafting, radiating, and other methods to produce or optimize desired traits.
- We know of nothing that stays the same indefinitely. Even inanimate objects change with time. Some fundamental particles exist for only billionths of a second, and some massive stars exist for billions of years, but all change. One of our most fundamental truths, the second law of thermodynamics, points toward change, and no exceptions have ever been found.

Even though evolution and religion are not compatible in many ways, it is hard to deny that evolution is real and has shaped and continues to shape life on earth. Other than the fundamentalists, who believe in a literal interpretation of Genesis, many religious people accept evolution and say it is God's way of achieving his end. Unfortunately, such thinking is tantamount to the intelligent design and fine-tuning arguments, both of which are meant to promote religion by saying God created or continually shapes the universe. Scientists define evolution as a random process where genes mutate and produce random anomalies and then natural selection picks the ones most favored. But even attributing evolution to God does not eliminate all the problems that evolution poses to religious beliefs.

One problem posed by evolution is that if humans have evolved from some previous form, the question arises as to God's image. Religious teachings indicate that God created us in his image. But if we are continually evolving, at what stage were we or will we be in God's image? It is not logical to assume that our existing form is God's image, because we have evolved for millions of years. And even if God created us only a few thousand years ago, as the fundamentalists believe, some change would have occurred during that period. If we accept evolution as fact, we must accept the premise that we may not presently be in God's image.

The bigger problem with evolution is the possibility that humans evolved from lower life-forms. If they did, when did they gain a soul or somehow become favored by God over other life-forms? And of course if humans evolved from lower life-forms, the biblical versions of creation are not literal. But that does not necessarily discredit the Bible for everyone because many feel that parts of the Bible, especially Genesis, are not meant to be taken literally. Only the fundamentalists would take issue with something other than a strictly literal interpretation. However, if you do not take the Garden of Eden part literally, then the original sin and all that it implies becomes moot, which triggers problems with other beliefs.

Also, if we evolved from lower life-forms, we must acknowledge that we are constantly evolving and will likely be in some other form in the future. This raises questions not only concerning God's image, as already mentioned, but also concerning the image or physical appearance of those in heaven. Will the residents of heaven look like primitive humans, present humans, future humans, or all? The only way to avoid these and other questions is to deny evolution, but denying a widely accepted scientific theory causes credibility problems.

Time, Place, and Copernicus

The ancients believed that the earth was the beginning of everything and was located at the center of the universe. This belief is evident in Genesis, which implies that the earth was formed before the moon, sun, and stars. And this belief is consistent with the belief that our religion explained everything in the universe. Logically, if earth was the first thing formed and was at the center of everything, then life and wisdom would originate and radiate from us.

Not until the sixteenth century did Copernicus theorize that the earth rotated around the sun, and Galileo was accused of heresy by the Catholic Church in the seventeenth century for defending the Copernican theory. Copernicus and Galileo thought the sun was the center of the universe because the planets rotated around it. However, present-day astronomers do not even give the sun a special place. Their observations indicate that our sun is just one of billions of stars in our galaxy and occupies no special place, and indeed our galaxy is just one of billions of galaxies in the visible universe. Also, evidence indicates that the earth was formed billions of years after the universe began, so we are neither at the center of everything, nor were we formed at the beginning.

In short, since the time God was defined, our understanding of our relationship to the rest of the universe has changed drastically. God was defined when we thought we were the beginning of everything and at the center of everything. God was defined when we thought life on earth was the only possible life in the universe. If we now recognize that the earth was not here first and that we hold no special place in the universe, and if we now accept even the possibility that life could exist elsewhere, we are faced with the possibility that our God may not be universal.

Lead Me Not into It
Temptation is the enemy of devoutness.

> Most people can be religious when temptation is removed.

Many temptations lessen with age. We do not necessarily get more devout. We just have less energy.

Many are tempted. Few are devout. No one is perfect.

Copernicus Revisited

Copernicus not only challenged the premise that the earth was at the center of the universe, but he also changed the way we define reality. Before Copernicus, reality was pretty much defined by religious and philosophical opinion. But Copernicus studied the movement of celestial bodies, and based on his observations, challenged the beliefs of his time. He paved the way for future generations to use observations and experiments to determine reality. Galileo built on the work of Copernicus and gained fame by openly challenging the teachings of the church. Isaac Newton continued the use of observation and experiment to develop his basic laws of motion and gravity, which are mathematical representations of reality.

Copernicus initiated the process of using observations and experiments to determine reality, and a similar process is still followed today. Today we demand physical evidence to justify a new finding, and then we want verification from multiple independent sources. We know that whoever makes the first observation or conducts the first experiment may have a personal interest in the results; therefore, we are reluctant to accept the outcome until we get independent confirmation. We want to see others make the same observations or conduct the same experiments to see if they reach the same conclusions. And if they do not, we will not accept the new finding. Einstein's theory of relativity is an example of a correct theory failing to gain general acceptance for many years because others could not verify it. In short, we demand a process of observation and experiment, much scrutiny, and ample verification before we accept any definition of reality.

That is not the case with verifying the existence or absence of God. Observations and experiments are not available to promote belief in a god or gods. Testimonials, opinions, and declarations are abundant, but observations and experiments or independent confirmations are not. God-based religions rely on ancient books, religious rhetoric, and missionary work to promote their beliefs. That in itself is not necessarily bad because the followers of such religions are entitled to their beliefs and have the right to promote them with whatever methods they choose, unless such methods cause harm. But without concrete evidence based on objective, empirical methods of proof, the validity of their beliefs is questionable. Many of us just cannot accept any definition of reality that is based on anecdotal evidence.

Little Green Men and the Bible

Scientists estimate there are billions of planets in our galaxy that could support life. They used four years of data from NASA's orbiting Kepler telescope to compute how many Earth-size planets lie in their solar systems' "Goldilocks zone," defined as the location where water would be in the liquid state on the planet's surface. Multiply those billions of planets in our galaxy by the billions of other known galaxies and you get an extremely large number of planets with the potential to support life. Admittedly these numbers are estimates and therefore are not exact, but even so, they show that there could be life elsewhere.

However, if it turns out that life exists only on earth, the creationists would have a good argument for the biblical version of creation. They could logically argue that if life really could begin anywhere the conditions are right, some other planets should be teeming with life. They could say the reason is because God created life on earth as stated in the Bible, and there is no mention of life being created anywhere else. On the other hand, if life exists elsewhere, independent of or preceding life on earth, then they have a big problem. Either way, given the vast distances in our galaxy, and indeed the universe, if we have to go there to find out, we probably will not get a definitive answer for a few million years. But keep in mind there is always the possibility that we will get a visit from one of those "Goldilocks" planets. If so, I hope the visitors do not have a god who tells them earth is the promised land and orders them to kill us and settle here.

What Is Life
Life is an interruption of nothing.

Gary L. Gaines

Life-after-Death Musings

Some physicists say no information is ever completely lost. They say all information is encoded in a digital or holographic or perhaps some other format that is so small and intrinsic as to be indestructible. If a book is burned, shredded, or otherwise destroyed, the information in it is not lost, and with the right equipment and know-how, it could be retrieved. Think of information as creating a lasting effect on the atomic, subatomic, and sub-subatomic waves and particles that make up the universe. Maybe someday, with the right decoder and ability to focus on a specific time, all information could be retrieved. This implies that even if a person died, was cremated, and had his ashes scattered over a wide area, everything about that person could be determined, and maybe even the person himself could be put back together with the right technology. Physicists think the key to that technology is quantum computing, or the ability to store and manage very large amounts of information, as large as the total number of particles in the universe. Although this line of thought is interesting, it is still pretty abstract, questionable, and at best a long way off.

However, along the same line in today's world, we know animals have been cloned. Tissue has been taken from live animals and used to develop replicas of the originals. This is old news now, but not so old are the efforts to replicate animals that are extinct, like the mammoth. Scientists are gathering tissue from long-frozen mammoths in the Siberian tundra with the thought of developing an embryo that could be brought to term in an elephant. Other extinct animals such as the passenger pigeon and Tasmanian wolf are also being looked at as possible candidates for revival.

The point of this discussion is simply to emphasize that we are manipulating life in ways never before thought possible. Genetically modified organisms and cloned organisms are present-day realities, and although the thought of cloning or resurrecting a human is hardly mentioned, the technology will likely be available some day. And this would not only be an astounding scientific achievement, but also one of paramount interest to the religious communities. How would religion deal with a cloned or resurrected human? I do not know, but we may need to start thinking about it.

Dating

Scientists use various techniques to determine the age of things. The techniques vary widely but generally rely on observing and measuring some natural phenomena. For example, the age of the universe is estimated by comparing the observed size of the universe with the measured expansion rate. The estimate is not exact because we do not know if the universe has always expanded at the present rate.

Other natural phenomena used to determine the age of things on earth include the radioactivity of certain materials, the layering of rocks, the deposition of fossils, the forming of tree rings, and many others. Many of the techniques are scientifically sound, widely accepted, and able to correlate with each other.

Various dating techniques indicate that the universe is approximately fifteen billion years old, the earth is a few billion years old, and life has existed on earth for over a billion years. These large numbers do not necessarily refute the Bible because parts of the Bible may be figurative and not meant to be taken literally. The large numbers do refute the fundamentalists who believe that the earth is only a few thousand years old. But more importantly, the large numbers provide a time frame that would accommodate natural processes of getting to where we are now. There would be enough time for the universe to expand and cool, for stars and galaxies to form, for planets to take shape and cool, and for life to begin in a very simple form and evolve to its present state. There are natural processes that can explain our present condition without the need for divine intervention, and dating shows us there has been enough time for the processes to occur.

A Quantum Fluctuation

> Nothing. Nothing. Nothing.
> More nothing.
> Continue nothing forever (almost).
> Then, blip, blip, blip.

An Agnostic's Path to God

Another blip.
Continue blipping forever (almost).
Then, bang, bang, bang.
Another bang.
Continue banging forever (almost).
Then, big bang!
Then, BIG BANG!
BIG BANG!

Time begins as mass, energy, and space explode from a point.
Hot plasma expands and cools, allowing matter to form and light to appear.

More expansion and cooling allow matter to cluster.

Gravity shapes the big picture.

Nuclear and electromagnetic forces shape the small.

Some clusters of mainly hydrogen contract and ignite nuclear fusion to form stars.
Some stars burn all their hydrogen, contract, and explode, forming heavier elements.
Multiple bits of various elements spin around some stars and coalesce into planets.
Some planets spin and cool in Goldilocks orbits.

Organic compounds start replicating on at least one planet.
The compounds grow in number and complexity.
Man appears, thrives, then disappears.

The universe continues to expand, cools, then finally disappears.
Time stops an instant after it started.

Quantum Quivers

Scientists attempt to explain reality. They develop theories to explain what they observe and what they believe to be reality. One of the most successful and comprehensive theories ever developed to explain reality is quantum mechanics. Quantum mechanics can describe with great reliability what happens on the quantum or very small scale. Our understanding of chemical and nuclear reactions and the development of transistors, atomic energy, nuclear medicine, lasers, computers, and the like, are evidence of the success of quantum mechanics. The particles and forces that exist on the smallest of scales could be thought of as the building blocks of the universe. Quantum mechanics has provided some insight into those building blocks.

In ancient times we thought everything was made from a few common ingredients such as fire, earth, and water. In modern times we determined that everything is made from about a hundred basic elements such as hydrogen, oxygen, and iron. We developed a periodic chart that lists the elements and provides details about the smallest units of each, which we call atoms. But even the atoms are not the basic building blocks of the universe. We have split the atoms and found smaller particles we call electrons, protons, and neutrons. We have even probed inside the subatomic particles and developed theories about sub-subatomic particles that we have given names such as quarks, gluons, and neutrinos. We are a long way from understanding all the particles and forces of nature, but we continually try to explain reality.

This discussion on reality is not meant by itself to discredit religious beliefs. If there is a god and he created the universe, he could have made it however he chose. But the discussion is meant to emphasize that details exist at all levels of physical reality, and to create the universe, God would have had to completely understand all the details, from the movement of planets, stars, and galaxies to the quivering of atoms, electrons, and quarks. Unfortunately, the religious books do not demonstrate such an understanding.

It Is about Time

Our understanding of time has changed. We used to think that time passed at the same rate under all conditions; however, Einstein showed us that time is relative. His work in the early part of the twentieth century showed us that time is related to space and velocity and can pass at different rates for different observers, depending on their relative location and movement. Without getting into the details, it is fair to say that Einstein's theories of relativity have been tested in many ways by many investigators and have always been found to be accurate.

Time is important to this discussion because there are timelines associated with a belief in God. Even for those who do not take the timelines in the holy books literally, belief in God is still related to time, and this is especially true for Christians and Muslims, since the lives of Jesus Christ and Muhammad have specific and fairly recent timelines. The equations developed by Einstein show that time differences in the universe can be great, especially for observers who are far apart or are traveling at hugely different velocities. Time differences of many thousands of years can exist at different parts of the universe, raising the question of the applicability of the theistic religions. For example, if other locations in the universe were thousands of years behind us in time, the timelines, writings, and beliefs concerning Jesus and Muhammad and even God would not have happened yet relative to any inhabitants of such locations.

To many, these comments will seem farfetched. Our minds are not used to thinking of time as being relative because we do not experience extreme velocities or distances. Velocity differences must approach the speed of light to have a significant effect on the passage of time for observers near the same location, and distances must exceed thousands of light years to leverage big time differences for observers at different locations. For the velocities and distances we experience in everyday life, the slight differences in time go unnoticed. But the theories of relativity rank among the greatest insights in the history of humankind, and countless experiments and observations have shown without fail that Einstein's equations are an accurate reflection of reality. If we accept that time is relative and that vast time differences can exist in the universe, we must question the universal applicability of religious beliefs that are related to specific timelines.

More Religious Bashing
Religion is an excuse not to think.

Religion divides us into groups and then drives the groups apart.

Religion is more divisive than race, gender, and sexual orientation; in fact, religion is the main reason those things are divisive.

Reading the Bible from cover to cover, not just the passages normally cited, will cause you to scratch your head and consider becoming an agnostic or atheist or maybe to just smile and ignore the parts you do not like.

Truth in the church is about as common as cleavage in the cathedral.

Religion's three *f*s: fear, faith, fantasy.

Religion is a virus.

Religions base a belief system on fantasy and then tout the beliefs as if they represent reality and defend the fantasy by saying we must have faith.

Religion defies logic, causing faith to be an emotion.

Religion is a salve for billions of people.

Most religious people are good, but most religions are not.

Time Revisited

The relative nature of time has been used to justify the timeline for the creation story in the Bible. The logic is that the reference point for the six days of creation referred to in Genesis is the instant the universe was created, and time passed much faster then. As the universe expanded and cooled, time passed slower and slower, until we reached the present rate, which began when humans were created. Think of biblical time as having two points of reference: the first six days being referenced to the instant of the big bang, and the remainder being referenced to the appearance of humans. The six days of creation are not days as we know them but eons. They are comparable to our days when viewed from the perspective of the hot early universe.

There is some logic to this premise because the passage of time is relative. Time passes at different rates for different observers based on the influence of gravity, location, velocity, and perhaps the expansion of space or other factors. Maybe time passed much faster in the hot early universe as compared to now. Maybe the passage of a day now would be equivalent to the passage of millions or billions of years earlier. The logic has merit.

But there are flaws in the logic from a religious perspective. First, other parts of the Bible do not demonstrate such a subtle, in-depth understanding of physics.

Second, if the timeline stated in Genesis is based on the relative nature of time, the timeline is not universal. It is relevant only from our reference point, or the approximate here and now. This implies that the Bible, or at least a part of the Bible, applies only to earth since the appearance of humans, which means the contents of the Bible are not necessarily universal truths. In short, if we apply relativity to justify the timeline of the Bible, we may be proving that the Bible is not written from God's perspective but from ours.

And third, we do not know for sure that the universe came into existence at a specific instant. The big bang theory, which posits that there was an instant of creation and is certainly embraced by many cosmologists, is still only a theory. The evidence is convincing but not conclusive.

The Appeal of Evolution

The theory of evolution is just that: a theory. We do not know for certain that life began through natural processes in simple form and evolved through natural selection to its present form. There is a lot of evidence to support the theory, but there are gaps in the fossil record that are hard to explain.

There is a bias toward believing in evolution for those like me who try to apply logic to everything. It just seems logical that life began in a simple form and that the forms that are favored by the environment have an advantage. But we are not dealing in certainties. If the fundamentalists are right, God created life a few thousand years ago in pretty much its present form. Maybe God even put the fossils in place for some reason. But even if the fundamentalists have the wrong timeline, that does not necessarily mean that life as we know it evolved from simpler life-forms. It may just mean that God created life at a different time or in some way we do not know about.

Whether we believe in creationism or evolution, we must recognize that neither can be proven with certainty at this time. Those who believe in God have no trouble accepting that God created us. Those who are uncertain about God have more trouble explaining how we got here. But for those like me who try to apply logic and cringe at relying on the supernatural, evolution has more appeal.

Who Can You Trust
Do not expect those who are religious to be objective on religious issues. Do not expect those who are anti-religious to be objective on religious issues. Objectivity on religious issues is about as rare as a pope in heaven.

Genes for God
Could it be that we are genetically predisposed to be religious? Did prehistoric people with some type of religious belief have a better chance of survival than their non-believing peers? I believe there are at least three reasons why this might be true.

Imagine prehistoric humans, with all the fears, dangers, and challenges they had to deal with, and you might conclude that the more careful they were, the better their chances for survival. Now, it follows that being very careful might make them accept rituals, superstitions, or the like, just to avoid the potential risk of offending the gods or spirits or whatever supernatural forces might be imagined. Second, religious people might be better able to deal with stress because of the comfort they find in their beliefs. Some religious rotes, rituals, and traditions are akin to meditation, which has been shown to be effective in stress reduction. And third, maybe prehistoric religious people would sometimes kill their non-believing peers in religious wars, rituals, rites, or terrorist activities.

If any of these reasons is true, then the most careful cave dwellers, or the ones who could best deal with stress, or indeed the ones who were not as apt to be killed by their neighbors, would likely live the longest and be more likely to pass along their genes. Therefore, modern people would be genetically programmed to be religious, even if the driving forces for passing on the genes have changed.

If we are genetically inclined to be religious, that would help explain why such a high percentage of us profess to be religious, even if we do not practice it. Maybe we have an underlying need to be religious or at least to profess religion. It would also help explain why so many of us can accept the supernatural based on faith. If we have an underlying or subtle need to be religious, maybe it helps block the logic we might otherwise apply in defining or accepting reality. Indeed, maybe we are genetically unable to be completely objective about religion.

More on Hardwired for Religion

Did we evolve to accept without question what our parents and other authority figures said? When the world was a much more dangerous place, it is logical to think that the children who did as they were told without question or hesitation were the ones most likely to survive and pass along their genes. Children who thought outside the box or questioned the logic of what they were told would be more vulnerable to the dangers of a hostile environment. Therefore, our minds evolved to a certain extent to put direction above logic when it came from authority figures, especially at a young age. That is why most religious people have the religion of their parents, and that is why they accept the dogma, even if it goes against logic. Natural selection has programmed them to do so. As an aside, many of today's children likely would not survive for long in a world where survival required a high degree of obedience.

What about Tomorrow

There have been many religious prophets, and some people point to certain events and say they were predicted by the prophets. For example, Christians point to the life of Jesus and say that many of the events surrounding his life were predicted by earlier parts of the Bible. However, there is not general agreement as to what was prophesied and what came to pass. Many of the prophesies are vague, and their meaning can be taken in different ways. And many of the events that are thought to be prophesied are debatable as well. I think it is fair to say that religious prophecies are generally embraced by the particular religion they apply to and are questioned by others. In short, they are not accepted as universal truths.

Scientists predict the future all the time. In fact science is based to a large extent on predicting future outcomes. I know there is a big difference between predicting the coming of a messiah and calculating the trajectory of a rocket, but both are about predicting future outcomes. And whereas many do not accept religious prophecies, few doubt the ability of science to regularly and reliably predict future outcomes in physics, chemistry, biology, math, astronomy, medicine, and so forth.

Admittedly some scientific theories, like the theory of evolution or the big bang theory, are not universally accepted, especially by the religious community, but those are more theories about past events instead of predictions about future ones. Whether or not we evolved from lower life-forms, or whether or not the universe began with a big bang, the ability of science to predict future events is accepted and used regularly, whereas the ability of religious prophets to predict future outcomes is largely a matter of personal faith. Logic tells me that science is a better tool than religion when it comes to talking about tomorrow.

Laws of Nature
As best as we can tell, the laws of nature are the same throughout the universe. Based on observations and measurements

from earth and from space, we have learned that the speed of light, the laws of gravity and motion, quantum mechanics, the expansion of space, background radiation, and other observable properties related to mass, energy, and motion appear to follow the same rules everywhere. This is remarkable! And it is an indication that everything began from one place or event.

If God created the universe, it is logical to think that the laws of nature would be the same everywhere, because they would all have originated from a single action. The same could be said if the universe was created from a single point by a big bang. However, there is a subtle difference. In a God-created universe, the laws of nature would be arbitrary; that is, they would be as God chose them to be. But in a big-bang created universe devoid of God, the laws of nature would be natural; that is, they would be the way they had to be as a result of natural events. Right now, we cannot tell the difference.

Digital Musings

Our world is going digital. More and more information is being transmitted, manipulated, and stored in digital form. The letters, numbers, punctuation, spaces, images, sound, and so on, in the information are being converted to on and off pulses called binary code we represent with zeroes and ones. Microcircuits containing tiny switches and other devices can manipulate the code to do almost anything our brains can do, only better and faster. Will digital reality someday compete with reality as we know it?

Certainly, it will get closer and closer. We already have artificial intelligence that can beat us at chess, *Jeopardy*, and many things involving information management. We already see and read fiction about living in a digital or virtual world. Before we clone or fabricate humans by manipulating DNA, we will probably create humanlike robots using digital technology. If we do a good enough job, they will be superior to us in many ways, especially as far as survival is concerned, because they will not be as vulnerable to environmental extremes and changes as we are.

It is possible that we will create robots in our image that can think, are self-sustaining, and can survive in a hostile environment. It is also possible that humankind will disappear due to natural or man-made catastrophes, and only the robots will survive. They may even create digital representations of themselves that have a consciousness and pull energy from celestial bodies for survival, eliminating the need for maintenance. If that happens, thousands of years from now, I wonder if they will look back upon us as gods. We created them and we kicked them around, but they survived and thrived. And maybe, much later, they may even look upon us collectively as God.

A Word about Consciousness

Scientists tend to analyze things from the bottom up. They examine the smallest units possible to try to understand the whole. Theologians tend to look at things from the top down. They look at all the units combined or the whole for understanding. Scientists deal in particles, matter, or the physical side of things, and theologians deal in the transcendental or spiritual or the nonphysical side of things. Scientists think that things are the sum of their parts, and theologians think that things are greater than the sum of their parts because of God. The bottom-up method is called reductionism and the top-down method is known as holism.

The two methods come into play when we try to understand consciousness, and there are many questions regarding consciousness that we cannot answer:

- How does consciousness work?
- How are we conscious of ourselves, our environment, and the past, present, and future?
- Do other animals have a consciousness, and if so, to what degree?
- How is consciousness related to language?
- At what point in our lives do we develop a consciousness, and at what point in our evolution did we develop one?
- Is consciousness the result of divine intervention, or is it the result of our brain acquiring knowledge and experience and using that to create awareness?

The exact mechanism of consciousness is unknown, and how we define it depends a lot on our religion or lack thereof.

If consciousness is a product of divine intervention, then it could be viewed in two ways. The theistic view would be that we have a god-given consciousness, and he controls it, in which case we may not have free will. The deistic view would be that God gave us a consciousness, but allows us to control it or exercise free will. Either way our whole would be more than the sum of our parts because of the nonphysical or spiritual part that results from divine intervention.

If there is no divine intervention in our consciousness, then it results from the physical makeup and activity of our brain and body. As we evolved bigger brains and became better able to acquire and process information, the input from our bodily senses made us more aware of our condition, and we developed a consciousness. Even though the mechanism of such a consciousness is unknown, there are reasons to think that our consciousness is free of divine intervention.

First, consciousness generally increases with age. Babies have little, children have more, and adults have the most. This implies that consciousness is related to our life experiences, which are different for every person. Second, consciousness seems to be related to intelligence. The great thinkers of the past (Copernicus, Newton, Einstein) experienced a similar reality as their peers, yet they had a more revealing or in-depth consciousness of it. They were aware of and could describe phenomena that others did not or could not. And third, consciousness diminishes, disappears, or changes under certain situations, such as when we sleep, are under anesthesia, suffer from dementia, or die. None of this is proof that consciousness is a manifestation only of our minds and bodies, but certainly it is not the same as the concept of the soul, which most religions believe is similar for everyone and remains viable after death. Perhaps all that can be said for certain is that if divine intervention is involved in our consciousness, the intervention varies from time to time.

I believe consciousness is a manifestation of physical activity in the body. I think it is similar to intelligence in that it is related to brain development. We are born with a brain, and as we gain intelligence and experience, we develop a mind with a consciousness that is unique to each individual. The physical process of gaining information through our senses and storing it in our brain increases our awareness and allows our mind to develop. If indeed the process is a physical one, there is no need for divine intervention. But until consciousness is fully understood, a strong argument cannot be made as to whether it is a manifestation of physical activity in the body or a result of divine intervention. However, logic tells me that consciousness is not dependent on any god.

The Next Challenge
Religion says humankind is special. Copernicus challenged that by pointing out that we are not at the center of everything. Darwin challenged it again by saying we evolved from

lower life-forms. Perhaps the biggest challenge would be if we encounter alien life-forms. But the next big challenges are likely to come from cloning and artificial intelligence. Both have already been discussed, so I will just say that I think AI will cause challenges before cloning does. Humans could probably be cloned within a generation, however strong public opposition will likely prevent it. But advancements in AI come incrementally and happen more to machines in a technical setting, so they occur without being noticed by the general public. Nevertheless, when we wake up one morning and realize that computers are a thousand times smarter than we are, have a consciousness, and can self-replicate, we will have to wonder about the religious implications.

The Logic of an Agnostic

Muslims deny the Christ, Christians deny the Prophet, Jews deny both, and agnostics deny knowing.

Muslims look to the Quran, Christians have the Gospels, Jews revere the Torah, and agnostics deny knowing.

Muslims pray to Allah, Christians say Jesus is Lord, Jews have the God of Moses, and agnostics deny knowing.

Muslims say Allah is one, Christians say God is three, Jews say three is heretical, and agnostics deny knowing.

Six

What I Believe

As an agnostic, I do not accept the deity of the Bible or the Quran. I do not rule out the possibility of a god, but I am not convinced one has been identified. It is important to understand that I do not believe this way because I want to. I believe this way because it is where my logic takes me. I would welcome the promise and security that believing in an omnipotent god provides, but I just cannot believe in something my logic denies.

Nonetheless, I do have specific beliefs on various issues. They do not stem from religion but are core values, basic truths, or principles I have come to accept. The following are some of the things I believe. They are categorized in an attempt at organization, but some do not fit well in any of the categories.

Moral Issues

We should respect others. Not only should we respect others, but we should try to live our lives such that others respect us and we respect ourselves. Activities that diminish respect include:

Murdering, raping, dominating
Violence in word or deed
Lying, cheating, stealing, hating
Deviance, coveting, greed

Many of these activities are related to the nontheistic parts of the Ten Commandments.

Promoting mutual respect is also related to the golden rule, the concept of treating people the way you want to be treated, some form of which can be found in almost all religions.

We should not exploit animals, especially those that have a consciousness and feel pain. We should avoid activities that contribute to the suffering of such animals. Our treatment of animals tells a lot about us since we have power over them.

We should respect and protect the environment. We should not pollute our neighbors or leave pollution for others to clean up. Our treatment of the environment tells a lot about us since it speaks to future generations.

We can discover and defend the basic principles of morality through logic and reason. There is no compelling need for divine guidance.

Only lower life-forms have sex without love.

Abstention is the best form of birth control, and abortion is the worse.

Monogamous unions between a man and a woman are best; however, same-sex unions are acceptable if the participants are so inclined.

Our actions are more telling than our words.

Social Issues

We should value freedom, diversity, and independence.

We should teach our children to question everything and to think objectively, logically, and empirically.

We should help those who are in need but recognize that too much help can undermine independence and create a group with expectations beyond what is good for its members and for society in general.

We are born with a brain, and as we gain consciousness, intelligence, and experience, we develop a mind. The brain is an organ that stores information, and the mind is that part of the stored information that defines us as individuals.

The family is the most important unit and should be put ahead of other considerations. We should honor our families and care for them the best we can. Spouses and children come first, followed by parents, siblings, and extended family. If family members do not take care of each other, if they allow the government or others to provide the care they need, the family structure is threatened and family ties diminish.

We must think logically, objectively, and rationally to reach the truth. The closest we come to a technical truth is when analytical investigations by multiple independent investigators produce the same or similar results over and over.

Most of the information we get is biased. All levels of government are routinely disingenuous when called upon to defend their actions, and many government agencies disseminate propaganda to sway public opinion. The media often embellish or spin the news in hopes of improving ratings. Many politicians lie to gain favor, businesses put profits ahead of stated goals, friends and family are seldom objective, and churches always promote a self-serving point of view. Be leery of information from biased sources and remember that all sources are biased.

Personal Issues

Eat regularly. Eat in moderation. Do not routinely keep eating until you are full. Eat mainly fruits, vegetables, and grains. Do not eat animals.

Get enough rest on a daily basis. Following a routine is beneficial.

Clean the body thoroughly on a daily basis, practice good hygiene, and groom regularly.

Value and protect personal health and avoid activities that threaten health. Many health problems are related to obesity, alcohol, tobacco, poor diet, and a sedentary lifestyle.

Exercise the body vigorously for at least thirty minutes every other day and be physically active otherwise.

Constantly exercise and challenge the mind by reading, writing, creating, learning, planning, speaking, listening, and solving problems, and avoid a lot of passive mental activities such as watching or listening to man-made devices or sitting in church.

Apply sound logic, objective reasoning, and empirical facts to determine reality. Drugs, wealth, power, religion, ego, and other factors can distort the perception of reality.

Philosophical Issues

Knowledge is related to truth and should be sought with vigor and without prejudice. Knowledge is the key to living our lives in meaningful ways, but only if the knowledge is factual and objective; otherwise, we can experience a distorted reality, which can lead to inappropriate behavior.

Knowledge is the most enduring of our efforts and the best indicator of our condition.

The main difference between us and other animals is our advanced language skills, which includes math. Language allows us to communicate with each other in sophisticated ways. It allows us to reach a high level of awareness and to accumulate, store, and retrieve information. It even allows us to create fiction, such as *War and Peace*, *Moby Dick*, and the Bible.

The universe sprang from nothing and will eventually disappear, leaving nothing. This means time is an illusion; mass, space, and energy are borrowed entities; and ours is a transient reality, having no compelling need for divine intervention.

Our lives are influenced by random events that have no meaning of a religious nature.

More than anything else, God is an emotion.

An Agnostic's Path to God

Theology that conflicts with reality cannot stand.

A reward based on faith is denied to those who must have proof.

We should nurture a view of reality that is free of fantasy.

Freedom from religion is at least as important as freedom of religion.

Ancient documents that describe supernatural events and call for faith in a messiah who assumes multiple forms are bound to create confusion and conflict.

A supreme being is not required for life to have purpose, because intelligent life defines purpose (love, loyalty, empathy, joy, and so on).

A single truth is more important than a thousand beliefs.

Truth withstands all challenges. That is how we define it.

A supreme being worthy of love and admiration would be kind and forgiving and would not be manipulative, vindictive, self-serving, or needful of worship and sacrifice. If such a being wanted to tell us something, the message would be clear, powerful, logical, and fantasy-free.

Unquestioning faith is not a virtue and can lead to irrational behavior.

Belief in the supernatural requires that realty be ignored.

Many who embrace the Bible or the Quran have never read them or have views on them that were shaped primarily by others.

Greed, gluttony, coveting, and adultery are some of the accepted sins by many religious people.

Suicide is not a sin, unless done to hurt others. It is just a decision to stop living.

Beliefs that embrace human or animal sacrifice to atone for sin are flawed. It is not logical to think that a supreme being would promote the taking of innocent lives.

We have some free will, and the universe contains some chaos.

Life began when certain chemicals came together under certain conditions, and humans evolved from lower lifeforms. There is no compelling need for divine intervention.

A belief system that is based on the supernatural will be accepted in large part because of faith. Those without such faith will question the beliefs, especially the supernatural parts.

An Agnostic's Path to God

Our ability to contemplate our existence is related to our language skills.

Our inability to explain certain things is not proof of divine intervention, but is proof that we do not know everything.

Faith does not produce fact, and a lack of faith is not a sin.

A good god would value all people, regardless of their religion or lack thereof.

All religions cannot be right, and there is a chance that none are.

We fear death and want to make it less foreboding, so we rationalize by saying there is an afterlife.

We would be better off if religious differences did not exist.

Living a life of virtue is more important than embracing a certain belief system.

Life for most of us is good, and we are lucky to experience it.

Seven

What I Want

I have tried to explain why I cannot accept the Abrahamic god. I am not an atheist, because I do not deny the possibility of a god. I just do not think any have been identified. I think we should discard most of what we think we know about God and define him in a way that is truly godlike, because like most people, I would like for there to be more to our existence than the physical events of life. But I think the Abrahamic god has been so maligned and his religions so contorted that we almost have to start anew. I say "almost" because the non-proselytizing parts of the Ten Commandments, the golden rule, many of the words of Jesus, and some other doctrines are acceptable. But I want more.

I Want a God
I want him to be benevolent, omnipotent, omniscient, omnipresent, immutable, and personal. I want him to be happy

and to radiate love, goodness, and joy. I want him to be rational, forgiving, and kind. I do not want him to be a jealous god or to burn with anger. I do not want him to single out a chosen people or place but to value all people and places equally.

I want his message to be positive and direct. I do not want a message that includes the threat of a devil or hell or eternal damnation. I want his message to be clear, so we can know him and understand him without having to depend on ancient documents that are vague and contradictory and are manipulated by preachers, priests, popes, padres, and other pious poopheads. I do not want his message to depend on the words or actions of prophets, judges, or kings. I want such clarity that there will be no bickering over the meaning of his message.

I want a god who does not advocate or participate in genocide, homicide, or infanticide. I do not want him to use war or violence of any kind to promote his agenda. I want him to be tolerant of diverse people, ideas, and beliefs. I do not want him to make people a certain way and then condemn them for being that way. I want his way to be so outstanding, so superior, so obviously the right way that no coercion of any kind will be needed to convince us to be that way.

I want him to put goodness above worship. I do not want him to be manipulative, needy, or controlling. I want him to promote unity and harmony among all races and between people and animals. I want no talk of foreskins, animal sacrifices, or vengeance. I want no threats of punishment to the fourth generation or painful chastisement. I want no need to punish everyone for some original sin. I want no hate, pain, suffering, or evil. I want a god who can save humankind without having to torture and kill his son. I want a god who knows what I want.

I want his commandments to be less about religion and more about how we treat each other. I want commandments against slavery, child abuse, and discrimination. I want commandments against mistreating animals and harming the environment. I want him to make clear that how we treat each other, animals, and the environment has more significance than how well we follow pedantic religious rules.

If god chooses to resurrect the dead, I want a god who will not pick who he resurrects based on vague or arbitrary rules, meaningless controlling behavior, ceremonial rituals, or other criteria that can eliminate good people. I want a god who values all people and instills in them the behavior necessary to please him and be worthy of reward. I do not want a god who makes people a certain way and then withholds a reward from them for being that way.

I want a reality that is free of delusion, superstition, saints, angels, devils, supernatural events, and miracles. (I like fantasy in fiction, but not in reality.) I want happiness and security for me, my family, and all of humankind. And I would like for him to provide details on the beginning and structure of the universe, the nature of mass and energy, and the definition of time and space.

I want a god who makes me feel happy and secure when I talk to him at night before going to sleep. I want a god I can admire and respect. I want a god who cares for me. I want the best god I can imagine.

I Want a Religion

I want a religion that brings all people together instead of driving them apart. I want a religion that does not call for acceptance of illogical dogma. I want people to find joy in their religion, not hate. I want no rituals that call for animal sacrifice and no beliefs that hinge on human sacrifice. I want no pedantic rules, no false icons, no mind-numbing repetition, and no rituals involving blood, snakes, mind-altering drugs, or gibberish.

I want a religion that does not send out armies or terrorists to kill nonbelievers. The religion should be so compelling and appealing that the minds of nonbelievers can be changed with logic and promise, not fear and bloodshed. I want a religion that makes people happy, not scared, judgmental, angry, or pious. I want a religion that teaches love, not worship.

I want a religion that does not exploit the poor or the ignorant, that does not foster opulence, and that does not sell grace. I want a religion that is not commercialized, that is not run by a multitiered bureaucracy, that does not harbor centuries-old hate. I want a religion that is about harmony, understanding, joy, benevolence, happiness, and forgiveness. I want a religion that does not pontificate, excommunicate, or agitate.

I want a religion that is logical and empirical, not necessarily born of philosophy or mathematically provable, just devoid of illogical assertions and fantasy. I want a religion that does not depend on faith or false promises but on sound assertions and feasible outcomes. Religion should gladden the heart without ignoring the brain. Religion that ignores the brain cannot stand.

I want a religion that rational, sane people would design. I want rational, sane people to design a religion and for it to become reality.

I want a religion with a strong, powerful god who embraces strong, self-reliant people. I want the best of the God of Abraham without the dark side or the nonsense. I want the god and the individual to coexist and not be mutually exclusive. We must imagine a religion that is ideal and then make it happen.

I Want Heaven Too

I want everyone to go to heaven when they die. An eternity of hell or anything similar is an inappropriate punishment for anything done on earth. Maybe a limited time should be spent in some humane but undesirable place as punishment for certain activities and to facilitate repentance and then everyone should go to heaven. And heaven should be whatever each individual wants it to be, not some one kind fits all. I want heaven to know what each individual wants and make it that way.

Heaven may have to be an illusion, at least for some people, to avoid conflicts. But that is okay because then no physical reality would be needed to fashion heaven. It appears that all physical reality will come to an end some day in accordance with the second law of thermodynamics, in which case a heaven that does not rely on a physical setting would be good. In fact, unless there is a way to circumvent the end of physical reality, heaven will have to be illusory for everyone.

I want to be with some people, but not others. I cannot give names or specifics here, but heaven will know what I want and make it that way. I want heaven to offer meaningful work for those of us who need to be busy and feel useful. But these kinds of statements are really not necessary, because the heaven I want will know what each person wants and make it that way.

Gary L. Gaines

I want heaven to go on for as long as each person wants but to have the ability to change if the person wants. In short, I want heaven to be whatever each individual wants it to be, and I want heaven to know what each individual wants and make it that way. I want heaven to be ideal for all, which means it will be different for all.

Eight

What I Have

As kids, I think most of us wondered about the mysteries of life, but as we got older, we lost a lot of that curiosity—maybe due to the structure of our education system, the challenges of career and family, or the rote of religion and philosophy—or maybe we just got tired. But my curiosity grew, and as it did, I started questioning almost everything, especially concerning religion. And my questioning made me an agnostic.

My agnostic logic has pushed aside most of the traditional beliefs associated with the Abrahamic god, and I am becoming more focused on the god, religion, and heaven I want. This is not something that comes easily. Not only do I have to get past the beliefs of old, but I have to find logic and structure in the beliefs I want. My questioning of the traditional beliefs does help me get beyond them, but as I do, I cannot just turn on something I like better. I have to find and define a believable, logical basis for new beliefs. That takes a lot of time, thought, and imagination. But I have hope.

I am not a prophet (duh), although I do not really know what a prophet is or if a prophet knows he or she is a prophet. I am just a person who cannot accept the beliefs of old, and I try to figure out how the beliefs I want can become reality. We all need beliefs. We all need imagination. And I have hope.

I Have Hope

As I mentioned elsewhere, one of the most profound statements I have ever read posits that everyone experiences reality in a different way. The statement is attributed to different sources, so I will not try to name the source. I will just repeat it: "We don't see things as they are. We see things as we are." If that is right, and I believe it is, reality is a creation of our mind, based on our personal perspective. Of course, our perspective is influenced by the objective inputs we encounter, but still, at least part of our overall reality is fashioned by our minds and is therefore subjective to some extent, meaning my reality is different from yours, and yours is different from your mother's.

I believe the most objective reality we experience is the matter of the universe or the physical parts (atoms, molecules, planets, etc.), which exist independent of conscious thought. But I believe the nonphysical parts (religion, politics, emotions, etc.) are an extension of consciousness and are very subjective. In other words, we see the nonphysical parts as we are, and they would not exist if we did not. This means we create them with our minds or "as we are." I think god, religion, and heaven are perfect examples of "seeing things as we are." I see god, religion, and heaven the way I am, not necessarily as they are seen by others. And since there are so many different ways they are seen by others, it is apparent I am not alone.

This makes me happy because it gives me hope. I wrote this book for the most part to explain why I am an agnostic, but also to show that I am not an atheist or without hopes and beliefs related to a god. Admittedly, my beliefs are unique, but then so are the beliefs of many others. My beliefs are based on what I want, and truth be told, I think you could say the same about many other people.

I Have Imagination

The more I imagine and think about what I want, the more logical and real it seems. I feel imagination played a part, probably a big part, in the Abrahamic religions, maybe not so much in the roles of Muhammad and Jesus, but maybe more than most people think even with them. Nevertheless, imagination was at work, especially in the first and last parts of the Bible. Therefore, I do not believe it is sacrilegious or unprecedented to allow my imagination to enter in. I imagine a good god, a flexible religion, and a happy heaven for everyone. That cannot be too wrong.

And I truly believe that anything that can be imagined can become real, if not now, then years, centuries, or millennia from now. I believe our imagination created the beliefs that exist today, and I believe we can create better ones for tomorrow. If we would not accept flawed belief systems—if we wanted a god and a religion and an afterlife as I do and if enough of us felt that way for a long enough time—it would happen. I know our minds can create the reality we want. We can influence our destiny more than the god of our fathers can because in the end, "We see things as we are," and we can create the reality we want.

The Epiphany

I said in previous sections that belief in god is not a choice and that such belief does not make god a reality. I now think I was wrong, at least to a large extent. I now think that belief in god is indeed partly a choice and that such belief can make god a reality to the believer. I now think god and any associated religion and heaven are the reality of how we see things or how we believe. This is an epiphany for me. I have always been a realist, or someone who takes things as they are, believing mainly in the tangible and provable, not the transcendental or nonphysical. But now I see that some things, especially the nonphysical, are not as they are but as we are, and therefore our god does not have to be some rigid, inflexible entity but can be as we are too. Also, I now think that to some extent those who believe in god a certain way try to get others to believe the same way because they equate acceptance with reality. They think the more people who believe, the more real it becomes.

First, you accept or define a god. In the case of the Abrahamic religions, the god has been mostly defined by the Bible and the Quran, although each believer tempers that definition by how they are. Second, you try to make your belief stronger by getting others to believe. In fact, proselytizing is the cornerstone of Christianity and Islam. It is what Jesus and Muhammad and their followers did so well. That is why Christianity and Islam are the world's two largest religions, and that is why they compete on the world stage for followers. They focus on believing and convincing, sometimes in brutal ways, because the more who believe, the more real their religion becomes. It is all about the numbers.

With this epiphany I feel more confident than ever that what I want can and will become real. I have defined the god I want, and I am becoming more able to think in terms of that definition. I do not know if I want to try to convince others to believe as I do, but it does not matter. I believe that eventually others will come to the same or a similar conclusion without any proselytizing or preaching. In fact, I think others have already done so because they have been defining god in their own way for as long as belief in gods has existed. My epiphany is just now allowing me to understand that concept with logic and clarity. My epiphany is just now allowing me to catch up in a sense.

What about the Logic of an Agnostic

Does this epiphany mean that my logic regarding the Abrahamic religions no longer applies? After all, if we see things as we are, everyone believes something unique, and who is to say what is right or wrong, real or imaginary, when it comes to belief in a god? Who am I to say that my logic finds fault with someone else's belief? Well, I think there are enough differences between the Abrahamic god and the god I want that my criticism still applies. Here is my reasoning: The Abrahamic god is the god of the Bible and the Quran, admittedly modified to some extent by the belief of each individual believer, but nevertheless, largely defined by the holy books. Therefore, there are a lot of rules or dogma that are associated with that God, and that is where my logic finds fault. The god I want does not have any historical background or dogma to find fault with. And the major religions have used and continue to use questionable tactics to convert nonbelievers. In contrast, the religion I want could appeal to believers and nonbelievers alike based only on its merit. But most of all, the

An Agnostic's Path to God

Abrahamic religions have evolved such an unacceptable God and illogical belief system that a logical person just cannot help finding fault.

You Too Can Find a Path

A path to god is available to everyone. Christians, Muslims, and (some) Jews already think they have found it. But if we see things as we are, the path is available even to agnostics, secular humanists, atheists, or anyone else who does not accept the Abrahamic god. To be completely forthright, the path is not as explicit as the one with the Abrahamic religions. By that I mean there is not a rigid set of rules that pave your way to heaven. If you believe in and can accept the Abrahamic rules, stay with them. But if you have doubts and cannot accept the rules and associated dogma, consider another way. It is as simple as one, two, three:

First, catalog what you believe in. Give this a lot of thought because it establishes a value system to guide you. The catalog does not have to be extensive or literary or anything fancy. It is just a list of your core beliefs in your own words. It must be real. You must be honest. You must be able to read this list over and over, year after year, and say, "That is what I believe." And it goes without saying that the beliefs must not be antisocial, mean spirited, petty, and so on. They must reflect high moral principles and noble values.

Second, describe the god, religion, and heaven you want. Again, the descriptions do not have to be lengthy, flowery pages of prose. Just imagine what you think a benign deity should be like and put it in some simple words. If you have any background with the God of Abraham, you have a start. If you are familiar with the Bible or the Quran, you have a start. And with those starts, you also have some attributes you probably want to avoid. I know I did. That is the main reason I started this book in the first place. I just could not accept the God of Abraham. Oh, I could imagine him being omnipotent, omnipresent, omniscient, immutable, and so forth, but I could not imagine him being vengeful, desirous of animal sacrifices, needy, controlling, or willing to kill to get his way. In short, many parts of the Abrahamic god are very good, but not all, so I took the parts that I thought made sense and eliminated the parts that I thought were nonsensical or described god in an unacceptable way. I even added a little extra. You can do pretty much the same thing with religion and heaven. And I believe you will agree that none of what I said about the god, religion, and heaven I want would be offensive to any god.

And third, get comfortable with your beliefs. Understand that religion comes from the minds of human beings, and it can come from yours. You just have to lay the groundwork and then condition your mind to believe. Remember, we see things as we are, and when it comes to god, religion, and heaven, we can imagine them however we want them to be.

The only qualifier I can think of is similar to those above: be noble, be principled, have lofty ideals. When you start down the path to heaven, put your head in the clouds and keep it there.

And don't hesitate to edit what you have written from time to time, both your core beliefs and the god, heaven, and so forth, you want. As time passes, you will likely think of more core beliefs or different descriptors of what you want and may even have more revealing insight on some of the existing ones. If you continually edit the things you write, you will keep them accurate and relevant. A commitment to edit also makes you revisit what you have written periodically, which keeps it fresh in your mind. For me, writing and rewriting is paramount to discovering, defining, and refining my beliefs.

God Is

God is flexible. He can be many things to many people. He allows you to describe the god you want such that he reflects you. That is great! It gives you a personal god. And again, this is not inconsistent with fundamental religious beliefs if you acknowledge that God is described in many different ways in the holy books, from the God of Moses and David, to the God who sent Jesus and talked to Muhammad through Gabriel. If you compare the different manifestations of God in the Bible, the Old and New Testaments, and the Quran, they almost invite you to pick the attributes you want. This is a new way of looking at the concept of god, but I believe it is logical. If you believe that the holy books are the inspired word of God or are maybe just reflective of God's will, then you have to consider that maybe God in his infinite wisdom realized that he had to be many things to many people. Maybe it is part of the plan of Yahweh, Allah, and the Son of Man.

God is for you to define. It is not the events in life that define us but how we react to them. In other words, the actions we have some control over are more telling than the random events that trigger those actions. That is why the careful mental processes of cataloging what you believe and describing the god you want tell a lot about who you are. Some of us believe strongly in discipline and want a strict, judgmental god (the god of the Torah), whereas others may want a gentle, forgiving god (Jesus). Both preferences are right. When you define the god you want, there is no wrong, unless your definition does not represent the best you can imagine.

I need to be a little more definitive when I say, "There is no wrong, unless…" For any of this to be helpful, the god you define must be good. Only attributes generally thought of as good should be used. Remember, we want to get away from the negative attributes associated with the Abrahamic god. Also, the axiom of do no harm applies. God cannot be defined in any way that does harm to you or others. Finally, a good rule of thumb is to look to the holy books for help, either for what you want or what you do not want.

An Agnostic's Path to God

My God

When we create our god, we should make our creation plausible, or at least be able to imagine a path to plausibility by not violating the laws of physics; otherwise, we could veer into the illogical, which we are trying to get away from. (Note: The laws of physics, especially quantum physics, do allow for some seemingly impossible events, some of which are common and some, extremely rare.)

I do not want to use human pronouns or *it* to refer to my god in this section. (Human pronouns personify god, and *it* does not sound godlike.) Therefore, to avoid a cumbersome, tedious narrative, I will just state some of the beliefs and attributes that apply. My god has the following attributes:

- Is everywhere, like a wave or force field that spreads out over the universe. Loves the holy books as history and literature, except the parts where God is depicted incorrectly. Values all life, especially people, as shown by our being here. Has a consciousness that we cannot perceive. Records everything we say, feel, and think. Is the ultimate repository of all information about everybody and everything for all time. (We are immortal in the sense that all knowledge about us is never lost or destroyed.)
- Is without mass, maybe like the hypothetical graviton. We think gravitons are everywhere, and even though we cannot see them, we feel their presence.

- Came into existence with the universe and might have changed some as energy and mass evolved, space expanded, and time passed. (May have been the impetus that caused creation, although this can only be speculated.)
- Is omnipotent but rarely demonstrates this, in accordance with wave function probability. (Lack of intervention allows routine laws of nature to determine day-to-day outcomes. Chances are better for subtle, long-term intervention because prayer, thought, focus, effort, and so forth, increases likelihood of desired outcomes.)
- Is omnipresent (compare to a force field), omniscient (stores all information forever), and benevolent (no reason to be otherwise). Allows us to find logical answers and ignore illogical beliefs. Gives us a consciousness that guides us in determining right from wrong. For those who do not apply the guidance, adjustments will be made when they transition to the next state. (Will not exclude bad people, only bad behavior.)

(This was the hardest part of the book to write. Maybe I should have just said I believe and want what my god believes and wants and let the definition go at that. But that did not seem genuine. More was needed. More may still be needed, but I dare not go on.)

An Agnostic's Path to God

Where Is the Logic

Where is the logic in asserting that anyone can find a path to god? Actually, there are multiple reasons:

All religion comes from the minds of men. Some are thought to have been prophets, but who are the prophets? Men. And who has identified the prophets? Men. Of all the writings claiming to be the unaltered word of god, who has historically decided which ones become holy? Men. My point is that none of us can get the word of any god second-hand and be certain it is genuine. Maybe we are all prophets. I believe a personal god would interact with all of us in ways that allow us to form our own conclusions about him. Trust yourself. Form your own conclusions. Define a god you want, and rest assured the definition was divinely inspired.

And this is a common theme, but if there is a god and he is good, he would reward all good people. Actually, I believe he would see good in all people, even the ones we may think are bad. God would see the good, and he would remove any bad that might exist in their transition to heaven. God would not abandon any of his creations. He would know that all people have value and would not punish those who had not met certain standards. An all-powerful god would cleanse all people and make them worthy of heaven. Why would he do otherwise?

Could the real god be testing us with the Abrahamic religions to see if we would accept such a depiction of him? I do not believe so, because I do not think a true god would try to deceive us in any way, and tempting us with unacceptable religions would be a kind of deceit. But I can say the god I want would not behave the way the holy books describe; therefore, I do not want to think of him that way. I think he would be happy that I think of him as being everything good and nothing bad. I think that is completely logical and reasonable.

Why Do It

There are many reasons for creating a god of your own. First and foremost, most of us would welcome the comfort and security that believing in a supreme being or some kind of higher force could bring, especially if it is one we are comfortable with. We encounter many occasions in life when we need support: emergencies, catastrophes, death, and so on. It would be nice to have a ready-made mind-set to turn to. Personally, as an agnostic, I have always been reluctant to turn to god for support. It seemed somewhat hypocritical, but now that I have figured out the god I want, I feel much better about doing it.

Another good reason is that self-analysis is good for self-improvement. And to catalog what you believe in and describe the god you want requires a lot of self-analysis. It forces you to determine your values, priorities, and standards. It forces you to think about who you are and what you are comfortable with as far as religion is concerned. Inevitably some will want strong, controlling gods with prescriptive religions, and some will want just the opposite. In any case, self-assessment is good for you, and the process can make you a better person.

Many religions have strong proselytizing efforts and having your own beliefs would help insulate you from them. I am not necessarily saying that learning about multiple religions is bad. I am just saying that without consistent beliefs of your own, they can be confusing. Strong, stable people have well-defined beliefs and are not vulnerable to false or topical thinking. Also, strong people can articulate their beliefs, not necessarily in speeches to others but in talking to themselves.

Religion is mental. Having organized, well-thought-out religious beliefs is good for the mind. It shows discipline, structure, and strength. It shows you are willing to face the big picture and develop a philosophy of your own. It shows you have assessed religious thinking and are unwilling to accept flawed logic. That is not easy.

If more of us did this and shared our views, we could learn a great deal from each other. Eventually, I believe we would develop some universal beliefs and wants, putting us on a common path to making them a reality. Remember, the mental part of reality becomes stronger with use. Indeed, many of the Abrahamic faiths point to popularity as evidence of truth.

What It Means
It means you believe there is more to life than just the physical reality you experience, and yet you cannot accept the Abrahamic god of the Bible and the Quran; therefore, you have decided to create a god of you own. Other names for your creation would be okay, but *god* fits well because it carries the appropriate physical and transcendental meanings. The god you create has the attributes you value, and to the extent you can, you should try to emulate them. Creating the god you want is a serious matter, not to be done on a whim or taken lightly. It is a life-changing event, perhaps comparable to what a baptism is to Christians, what the hajj is to Muslims, or what a bar/bat mitzvah is to Jews. It must be well-thought-out, deliberate, and sincere. The basic process of creating is the easy part. Being like your creation over time takes commitment, discipline, and dedication.

Creating the god you want is about many things, and by far the most important is self-improvement. The god you create is a reflection of your core beliefs, and although he may have supernatural powers, he reflects your values. And any attribute of a human nature you want your god to have, you should try to have too, because this is not just about defining and structuring beliefs and wants; this is about defining and structuring you. Your core beliefs are important, and the god you want is important, but only to the extent that you commit to honoring what you want by being what you want. We see things as we are. We are what we believe. To be the best takes commitment and discipline. And you can do it yourself. In fact, only you can do it. Be the future you want.

Creating your own god is unlike other beliefs in which you follow some preset, rigorous guidelines. It is more like an awakening or realization or epiphany. You realize there is more, and you feel it is okay to see that more as you are. And then you try to live up to that more by being the best person you can be. Simple. Elegant. Sublime.

East Meets West

As previously discussed, Abrahamic religions teach us to look to an omnipotent god for answers, while many Eastern religions teach us to look within ourselves. I think it is relevant and interesting that my path produced a god that is manifested by looking within. I feel good about this because it allows me to have the god I want by combining what I think is the best of both worlds.

This East-meets-West idea is the essence of what I want and have. I did not think of it until I had the epiphany about seeing things as we are and creating the god we want. Maybe in a way I have come full circle: I have criticized the

Abrahamic religions but now combine them with Eastern thought to get what I want. In looking back it seems I applied a lot of thought, soul searching, writing, and imagination to get to such a simple idea, probably an idea that many people have been applying for millennia.

What about the Churches

There are reasons why some church people will not support the idea of creating your own god. They are devoted to their own beliefs and will not go along with opposing views. This is not meant as criticism, because being devoted to one's beliefs is not necessarily bad. Some may see this as heretical and not to be tolerated. And many church people will just oppose a different way of thinking on principle. Again, this is not meant as criticism. Many people go to a church because they agree with the church doctrine or something about the church, so it is natural that they would oppose conflicting points of view. And probably some, especially those in the church hierarchy, would oppose anything they think might weaken the church.

But I believe many people who go to or belong to churches would see this as a good thing simply because it would bring more people closer to god—maybe not to their fundamental or historical god, but arguably an arbiter of good nonetheless. They would realize that any time you can get people talking about or embracing even the concept of

An Agnostic's Path to God

god, it is a good thing. And as time went by, maybe more people would find some commonality in their gods, making this whole idea a unifier of fundamentalists, humanists, agnostics, and others.

And more importantly, this could be a path to survival for churches. Most churches are locked into frozen, ancient belief systems that become more outdated with time. As most of this book argues, the centuries-old attempts to define god are illogical. I know that universal truths are timeless, but the Abrahamic religions are about as close to universal truths as the pope is to Pluto (the dog or the planet). Truth is reality tempered by time, and if churches think that eternal truths were discovered centuries ago, never to change, then I fear they are denying logic and are doomed to slip even deeper into oblivion.

I think certainly the power and influence of the Abrahamic religions will fade as people become enlightened. I am not talking about god. As I have said elsewhere, belief in one god or another is widespread and steady. I am saying that belief has changed and will change more, and the only way a religion will stay relevant is to recognize and embrace the change. Those who do not may find solace in their loyalty, but they will also find a thinning congregation. Religion must be dynamic. Seeing our own personal god as we are is dynamic. For many, seeing god as we are will be tantamount to seeing the god of the past and the future. And seeing god as we are may open the doors of the churches to agnostics and others who would not otherwise attend.

Should those who create their own god join or form a church? I do not know. I am not antichurch, but I fear many churches lose sight of what is important. They get too caught up in their own dogma or worried too much about their popularity or survival. Personally, I prefer praying alone. And I do not like being tied to group thinking of any kind. But everyone is different. Some churchgoers have created their own god and do think independently, and they are to be praised. Honestly, I think a lot of people enjoy interacting with others who share similar religious beliefs; therefore, their churches serve them well.

Summary

We fear the unknown. We fear death. We seek protection from those fears, and religion provides that protection for many people. However, if religion becomes something other than protection and love, beauty, solace, and peace, it becomes part of the problem by creating fear. I believe the Abrahamic religions are part of the problem. My solution is to create beliefs that are not part of the problem. Beliefs that contribute to the dark side of humanity are not to be revered.

Matter exists independent of consciousness. Abstract things like religion, politics, and emotions exist as a result of consciousness. Consciousness is a human trait; therefore, humans create god, religion, and so forth. And since we cannot be completely objective, we create the abstract things in large part as we are; thus, in essence, we create the god, religion, and heaven we want. I have consciously worked in that direction, first by arguing against the God of old and then by trying to define the god I want. I believe my logic is sound, and I suspect a lot of people have, either consciously or unconsciously, done something similar.

To argue that the God of old is more real because he is based on the Bible and Quran is compelling. The Bible and Quran are documents that supposedly came from the God of Abraham, and if they did, their influence is rightly paramount in creating the god we want. And even though I have described a lot of illogical thinking associated with the Abrahamic god, there is sound thinking too, and some of that had an influence on me when I talked of the god I want. I believe if you consider all the many religions and beliefs associated with the Abrahamic god, you will agree that the god I want is not so unorthodox. In fact, my intent was to reflect all that is good about the Abrahamic god with none of what I view as bad or illogical or ungodly.

I have a god, I practice religion, and I want to go to heaven. But I cannot embrace a belief system that I find illogical or wrong, so I have described my own. My beliefs were created in my mind but were greatly influenced by the Abrahamic god. I have tried to explain why I believe as I do—not to diminish other beliefs but to show why I am an agnostic and how I have found a path to god.

An Agnostic's Path to God

My path was long. I have been an agnostic for many years, and as this book shows, I have many reasons for being one. But my path went in a different direction when I had the epiphany about not seeing things as they are but as we are. I realized that we can create the god we want and find comfort with him. This is such a basic and obvious realization that I am sure many have had it before me. And I suspect many more practice it without purposely setting out to do so or even realizing that that is what they are doing. I truly believe god is something different for everyone. Everyone's mind creates a different god. That is okay. That is how it should be.

We must leave the days behind when we argued about the definition of god. We must quit fighting over matters of religion. We must embrace the god that unifies. We must look with suspect at rigid religious practices that divide. We must quit proselytizing and start harmonizing. We can. I know we can. I think it is part of the plan of Yahweh, Allah, and the Son of Man.

Nine

What I Think Is Next

First the electrons were choreographed with matter to produce desired outcomes. Then just bits of matter were made to dance the dance. Finally, no matter was needed. The trick was done with mathematical structures. Information could be stored, manipulated, retrieved, and made real inside such structures. No need for matter, energy, space, or time. The mathematical universe was the final and everlasting home for all life that had ever existed. No life was lost. No information was lost. It all transitioned from matter to structures instantly without need of magic, messiahs, or more matter. It was a natural and inevitable process. Was it an extension of the last instant of life, when time stands still forever, or a mathematical reality called heaven? It does not matter. The results are the same. All life and everything that makes it real keeps on going forever. We made this happen with our minds. It can be done.

It started with life—namely, with data management via biochemical processes. It progressed with data management by means of manipulation at the molecular level. It advanced to the quantum level and reached its pinnacle with mathematical structures. The progression was logical and inevitable, needing only matter, energy, space, and time until the structures were perfected. The material world gave us the matter, energy, space, and time, and our mental prowess did the rest.

Everything we know, feel, see, hear, touch, or otherwise sense is in our brains. All of history as we know it, all of life's experiences, all of our reality is in that one-liter volume of brain cells. To us as individuals, the world, galaxy, universe, and anything more is in our brains. We are essentially our brains. And you do not even need the organic cells and mechanisms with all their intricacies that make up your brain to define you, just the information it contains. So you do not have to recreate or retrieve everything, just the information. Simple as pi. Bits and bytes. Mathematical structures. No matter, energy, space, or time needed.

We transition from a living, breathing existence to the same in a different format the instant our body falls. All of life's information and history is instantly coded into a mathematical structure that never dies because it is not dependent

An Agnostic's Path to God

on mass, energy, space, or time. And the structures dance in a heaven that also needs no mass, energy, space, or time. Of course, we perceive reality. We do not bemoan the mathematical structure because being is reality, regardless of form.

Hindsight helps us understand God:

God is information. No information is lost. All information is made to last forever.

God is good. All information is tweaked to allow everyone to go to heaven. No one is lost. No personality is changed. Only undesirable traits are smoothed in ways that make everyone happy.

God is choice. No one is left behind, and no one is made to do anything, including exist.

God is forever. Nothing lasts forever, except information. The only trick is managing it. Managing it is easy when obstacles are removed. Obstacles include mass, energy, space, and time.

This is the god we hoped for. This is the god we wanted. Life—and afterlife—are good!

In Every bad There is Good.

Epilogue

The drifting relaxed me as I floated on a warm, clear lake. The azure sky was spotted with puffy white clouds sliding toward the horizon. Along the horizon I could just barely see a yellow-and-green glow, and as I got closer, the glow turned into a lush green meadow spotted with bright yellow-topped daffodils. Beautiful. Tranquil. Great goodness—this must be it. No pain or anxiety remained. A smooth, quick transition. I knew it.

I could see the information spewing from the daffodils, bits gathering into bytes, which turned into Spot, a dog from my childhood, and then several running white-faced cows. Without hesitation I chased the cows through a field dotted with daisies, faster and faster, until I got in front and turned them toward the barn, Spot close at my heels. Whew! Cows in the barn. I love running. Running is living. Life is good.

The reality of life had transitioned into a different reality, simple and easy. The transition happened in an instant. Billions of years had passed in a blink after the transition gate opened. Old stars died, and new ones hatched; black holes exploded or evaporated, a particle at a time; galaxies whirled, collided, disappeared, and grew; space expanded faster than light; and energy, both bright and dark, always nebulous, spread out more and more. Ah, the energy—not new, only old and fixed. It was the spreading that pushed energy past its apex, past the place where it set things in motion, causing the whole shebang to start cooling, cooling, until the cool eventually penetrated the plasma and turned out the lights. Darkness spread, one by one. Some life died with its star, and some fled to another star and then to another, but ultimately, all vanished into the code of what was. It all happened very slowly and very fast, depending on your perspective.

All the information on everything for all time found a home, a permanent home, in mathematical structures, which contained nothing but the knowledge, the data, the information, the real god. This, the ultimate. I knew it. No change needed from here.

As my life passed before the floating me, I smiled with happiness and contentment. The bits fell in place, all of them, making it real. I knew all. I had all. Nothing could take this away from me except my desire to change. I had everybody and everything, and we interacted exactly the right way for me. Nothing could be better. I could walk, I could talk, I could see and hear. I was complete and content. Life was good. I knew it would happen.

Where or when or how did the march to mathematical structures begin? I think I know, but really I know only a tiny smattering. There is too much to know. But when people started turning, it became possible. People made it real. First a speck, then a dot, then a spot, and so on. We see things as we are; then, in time, they become that way. That made it turn. That made it real. I had thought so, but I was unsure. (It is not easy to be sure about something like that.)

The turning of the people brought the digital into play, which made the future possible. Bits, bytes, silicon, and then quantum particles made information the thing that shaped the future. As it got smaller and smaller, it got bigger and bigger, until it was so small that it got infinitely large. Fortunately, that happened before the lights went out, or maybe it would have happened anyway as the logical progression of things. I am not sure.

The machines took over. It was good and bad: good for progress, bad for egos. Many predicted the singularity, few believed, until it shot by so fast as to seem as if it had always been that way. Events flew after that. Smaller and smaller. Bigger and bigger, until most of the particles in the universe were being used, but before they ran completely out, the biggest discovery yet: mathematical structures. Hallelujah! To paraphrase a famous line from the cartoon character Pogo, "We have met the future and it is us."

Nobody is lost in the transition. The miscreants have a few bytes modified, easy as pie, and then they are as good as any. All the unborn come as children, and all the children are allowed to mature to adolescence before they decide. Some prefer childhood; indeed, many adults go back to childhood. It is what they want. Turns out, we all get tweaked to some extent to deal with varying degrees of racism, prejudice, envy, resentment, pride, and so forth. It makes us happy. Happy. Happy. No problems; happy fixes all. It is grand. It is all anyone had hoped for and more: streets of gold, in the lamb's fold, or something else entirely, as yet untold. Anything is possible.

We remember a little from before the transition, as if we had dreamed it or someone had told us about it. But it is no handicap. The reality makes it irrelevant. Everyone's reality is free of bad memories, envy, disappointment, loss, or other negative experiences. When you are living content and happy with everybody and everything you want and need, you just do not imagine another kind of existence. Occasionally, someone chooses to go away. That is okay. They can return another day. Information is never lost, and choice is always an option.

An Agnostic's Path to God

I saw a puppy dog wagging his tail, and that did away with the soul business. Well, not really. The soul turned out to be some form of zeros and ones that lasted forever in a format that required no mass, energy, space, or time. I am glad. I like puppy dogs, and I do not like fantasy when it comes to important, life-changing events. It is better to have things settled by nuts and bolts instead of the supernatural and make believe. You can count on nuts and bolts. It is the natural course of things: no miracles, no magic, no sacrifices. I like life without magic, especially without sacrifices—human, animal, or otherwise.

I work in dirt during the day and study at night. It is grand. It is what I imagined. I love dirt: digging, planting, and tilling especially, but smelling, smoothing, and shaping too. I do not think I will ever get tired of dirt. I study as I did before, especially quantum stuff. It is of little importance now, but I still wonder. Dirt during the day; neutrinos, neutrons, and so forth, at night. Life is good. Or should I say, "Life after life is good."

If you want another landscape or season or to travel—no problem. Imagine it! And, yes, you can think about what you want without implementing it. Heaven knows what you want. Remember, we see things—other than those made from matter—as we are, and if there is no matter, that means everything. Maybe now we can say, "We create things as we are," or to paraphrase, "Things are as we are." Instead of having one wish or two or three, we have an infinite number. The genie never goes back inside the bottle. No one can imagine anything better. If someone could, it would be.

The sun shines as before—nights, days, seasons, weather—all just the way I like. But not to worry—multiple suns, constant days, and static weather are all available too. Life throughout the universe, multiverse, and parts beyond are easily accommodated without problems.

Our minds are stronger than anything else. What the mind perceives shapes the future. Everything else is secondary. Whatever the mind can perceive can become real. We see things as we are. We perceive things as we are. Life after life is just an inevitable extension of us. We are here. We are now. And our minds can shape the future such that we will be forever. All it takes is to believe it.

ABrahamic ⇒ Athiest

Printed in Great Britain
by Amazon